PRAISE FOR *VEGAN EATS WORLD*:

"*Vegan Eats World* is a worldwide culinary tour featuring some of the most imaginative vegan dishes I have ever encountered. . . . Romero's inspiration came from almost every corner of the planet. . . . The main lesson to be learned from this cookbook is that plant-based meals need not be bland or uninspired. The international recipes selected for this cookbook are not just healthy choices but also delicious ones. . . . I recommend this cookbook, regardless of whether you are a vegetarian. The recipes are accessible and innovative."

—TUCSON CITIZEN

"Romero plays culinary tour guide on a romp across the globe that sees scores of distinctive dishes filtered through a vegan spyglass. . . . Perhaps the greatest success Romero delivers is in making an interesting variety of vegan recipes accessible to the everyday home cook. Many of these dishes are the kind of thing you'd want to eat just because your palate was feeling curious, not out of adherence to any specific diet."

—WILMINGTON STAR-NEWS

"From vegan-queen Terry Hope Romero . . . [it] takes you around the world to spots as diverse as Jamaica, India, and the Philippines, through adapted dishes like a tangy Filipino-inspired tofu and vegetable adobo stew topped with chopped cilantro and bananas."

—FORBES.COM

"Jam-packed with 300 delicious recipes. This title takes you on a globetrotting journey to savour the best vegan cuisine the world has to offer. There are some wonderful combinations of ingredients used to create innovative dishes. . . . Terry's books are always well written and great value for money and *Vegan Eats World* is no exception."

—THE VEGETARIAN

"Not only are classics re-created but new dishes based on different, vegan ingredients are introduced, with recipes labeled for time and complexity. . . . [*Vegan Eats World*] is a pick for any who would incorporate vegan dining into a new worldview."

—MIDWEST BOOK REVIEW

"A masterful collection of . . . recipes from all corners of the globe. . . . [Romero has] reinvented delicious ethnic dishes, popular street foods, and take-out so we can eat well while being mindful of a healthy body and healthy planet."

—IRVINGTON HERALD

PRAISE FOR *VIVA VEGAN!*:

"*Viva Vegan!* hits the mark. Celebrating her Venezuelan roots—and Latin culture as a whole—the NYC-based chef has not simply veganized Latin-food. . . . Instead, she presents unique dishes infused with Latin flavors. . . . Thirteen well-organized chapters of recipes cover everything from quintessential condiments to more versions of rice and beans than you ever thought possible."

—VEGNEWS

"In Romero's kitchen, firm tofu is turned into a chewy, smoky pan-fried 'vegan stunt-double' for *chicharrón*, the fried pork rinds popular in the Caribbean, while ceviche is reimagined with mushrooms or heart of palms."

—NEW YORK DAILY NEWS

"Loaded with attitude to show that vegan cooking can be an absolute blast and doesn't have to rely on faux meats and pretend cheeses to taste good. . . ."

—PORTLAND OREGONIAN

"[Romero] comes to the rescue of cooks whose imagination limits their vegan output, and vegans who would like more Latin dishes on their menus. There is a great selection of dishes that everyone will enjoy.... 'Crepes with Un-Dulce de Leche and Sweet Plantains' are swoon-worthy.... Bottom Line: Would I buy *Viva Vegan!*? Sí."

—BLOGCRITICS.ORG

"What sets Romero's recipes apart from other vegan fare is her reliance on standard kitchen ingredients—not creepy faux meats.... Her recipes ultimately rely on fresh ingredients, creating healthier, lighter versions of otherwise traditionally heavy meals."

—SACRAMENTO BOOK REVIEW

PRAISE FOR *VEGANOMICON*:

"Spending time with [Moskowitz's] cheerfully politicized book feels like hanging out with Grade Paley. She and her cooking partner, Terry Hope Romero, are as crude and funny when kibitzing as they are subtle and intuitive when putting together vegan dishes that are full of nonsoggy adult tastes.... Do look for an excellent roasted fennel and hazelnut salad, bok choy cooked with crispy shallots and sesame seeds, hot and sour soup with wood ears and napa cabbage and a porcini-wild rice soup they say is 'perfect for serving your yuppie friends.'"

—NEW YORK TIMES BOOK REVIEW

"Exuberant and unapologetic.... Moskowitz and Romero's recipes don't skimp on fat or flavor, and the eclectic collection of dishes is a testament to the authors' sincere love of cooking and culinary exploration."

—SAVEUR

"[T]his slam-bang effort from vegan chefs Moskowitz and Romero is thorough and robust, making admirable use of every fruit and vegetable under the sun."

—PUBLISHERS WEEKLY

"Full of recipes for which even a carnivore would give up a night of meat."

—SAN FRANCISCO CHRONICLE

"It's no shocker that the very same urban chefs who had you inhaling vegan butter-cream frosting during your free time have crafted the next revolution in neo-vegan cuisine."

—PHILADELPHIA CITY PAPER

"*Veganomicon* not only offers tons of mouthwatering ways to put 'veg' back into your vegan diet with actual produce but also tutorials that gave me confidence to start improvising on my own."

—BUST

"*Veganomicon* is user-friendly, packed with tips and instructions for a wide range of cooking techniques."

—NEW YORK SUN

"The *Betty Crocker's Cookbook* of the vegan world.... It's one more step in the quest to prove that vegan food really doesn't taste like cardboard when you know what you're doing."

—BITCH

"Seriously good with broad appeal."

—WASHINGTON POST

SALAD
SAMURAI

ALSO BY TERRY HOPE ROMERO

Vegan Eats World

Viva Vegan!

WITH ISA CHANDRA MOSKOWITZ

Veganomicon

Vegan Cupcakes Take Over the World

Vegan Cookies Invade Your Cookie Jar

Vegan Pie in the Sky

SALAD
SAMURAI

100 CUTTING-EDGE, ULTRA-HEARTY, EASY-TO-MAKE SALADS YOU DON'T HAVE TO BE vegan TO LOVE

TERRY HOPE ROMERO

Da Capo
∞
LIFE
LONG

A Member of the Perseus Books Group

Designed by Megan Jones Design

Set in 9 point The Mix by Megan Jones Design

Cataloging-in-Publication data for this book is available from the Library of Congress.

First Da Capo Press edition 2014

ISBN: 978-0-7382-1487-0 (paperback)

ISBN: 978-0-7382-1752-9 (e-book)

Published by Da Capo Press

A Member of the Perseus Books Group

www.dacapopress.com

Note: The information in this book is true and complete to the best of our knowledge. This book is intended only as an informative guide for those wishing to know more about health issues. In no way is this book intended to replace, countermand, or conflict with the advice given to you by your own physician. The ultimate decision concerning care should be made between you and your doctor. We strongly recommend you follow his or her advice. Information in this book is general and is offered with no guarantees on the part of the authors or Da Capo Press. The authors and publisher disclaim all liability in connection with the use of this book.

Da Capo Press books are available at special discounts for bulk purchases in the U.S. by corporations, institutions, and other organizations. For more information, please contact the Special Markets Department at the Perseus Books Group, 2300 Chestnut Street, Suite 200, Philadelphia, PA, 19103, or call (800) 810-4145, ext. 5000, or e-mail special.markets@ perseusbooks.com.

10 9 8 7 6 5 4 3 2

TO HUNGRY
16-YEAR-OLD VEGANS
EVERYWHERE
OF ALL AGES

CONTENTS

INTRODUCTION:
A NEW SALAD MANIFESTO
(OR, STOP MAKING SALADS THAT SUCK)

"But there's always the salad."

If you don't eat meat (or any animal-derived food), ordering a meal in a nice, if not necessarily accommodating to a vegan palate, restaurant usually drifts to the inevitable rendezvous with a salad. Everyone tucks into steak and potato-flavored mounds of butter. You, however, poke your fork into a morose pile of limp leaves. As a teen vegetarian (and later, adult vegan), countless experiences like this one soured me on ever loving salad. Or actively seeking it out as a meal. Salads just sucked.

But a few cookbooks and decades later, my appetite has shifted increasingly away from cupcakes and casseroles to smoothies, soups, and yes . . . salad. But not the pale mounds of iceberg lathered in bottled dressing or its modern "upscale" accomplice: the pile of tasteless "spring" baby greens glistening in sugary, one-note "balsamic" dreck.

The real salads I crave and eat on a daily basis are hearty, genuine meals! They are true one-bowl wonders, beautiful unions of crunchy fresh vegetables and often fruit, that are always loaded with hearty plant-based proteins, freshly made dressings, and crunchy toppings that gild something much tastier than a lily. Best part yet: something that tastes this good doesn't even take long to make. Prepare a batch of dressing, chop some veggies, and pack it all up for memorable meals throughout the week.

If you opened this book looking for quiet, demure side salads, I'm afraid you're outnumbered (or just turn to page 30 for no-brainer suggestions for side dishes). These are generously proportioned entrée salads for big appetites! You may even need to buy a few new big bowls to contain these megasalads; no need to unpack the little plates and dainty salad forks.

Why *Salad Samurai*? Because you are the salad samurai, master of your salad-making domain! Don't worry, you're not required to live by some kind of vegetable bushido code. The only thing that we (as in all the vegans, vegetarians, and even omnivores in favor of meatless meals) must do is rescue salads from their sucktastic reputation as wimpy fare. *These* are salads to fight over!

PART 1

THE SPIN: THE SALAD SAMURAI CODE

SALAD SEASONS, SALAD DAYS

SALAD SEASONS, SALAD DAYS: LEAFY GREENS FOR FOUR SEASONS

In our culture, salads are typically associated with relief from cooking during the sweltering days of summer. But a colorful bowl of raw and cooked vegetables, grains, and proteins with the right toppings is a joy any time of year.

I love eating seasonally. I enjoy the hell out of peak produce! Hence, these recipes are organized into seasons. You must savor the plump, aromatic tomatoes of August, the sharp crunch of September apples, and the tender bittersweet glory of spring's first arugula. BUT, don't feel limited by my suggestions; many of these hearty salads are great throughout the year! You'll find your favorites among this recipe escapade of flavors and textures; the Vanessa Kabocha Salad (page 157) with its red cabbage and 5-spice peanut sauce and the BBQ Tempeh 'n' Dilly Slaw Bowl (page 107) are year-round habits of mine.

Not surprisingly, summertime salads outnumber all of the seasonal recipes. Summer heat and chill vibes ease us into cooking while savoring all the flavors of the bounty of the season. Hot, muggy weather leaves our palates longing for the sharper, acidic flavors of berries, vinegar, and citrus, or the juicy, water-filled relief of ripe tomatoes and heavy, fragrant peaches picked only yesterday.

But salads form the crux of my way of eating all year-round: as the weather cools, the combination of roasted veggies, still-warm cooked grains, and savory grilled proteins provides the perfect balance of vegetables and protein with less emphasis on filling starches. And hello, there's a world of roasted Brussels sprouts, pumpkin, sweet potato, and other mouthwatering winter veggies that can do serious time as salad accompaniments.

The last chapter, Sweet & Savory, favors bold breakfast palates. I must eat breakfast, but muffins and pancakes are weekend treats; I'd rather start my busy weekdays with nuts, whole grains, minimal added oils and sugars, and abundant fresh fruits, beans, or veggies. This little collection of breakfast salads (and smoothie bowls) is a foray into fresh, high-energy fare that powers me through the morning and well into the afternoon without a tummy rumble or need for a snack. Try them and see: I hope you enjoy the fruits (and veggies and grains) of my labor!

SALAD DAYS: PLANNING A WEEK OF SALADS FOR A DAILY DOSE OF EASY LIVIN'

Hard-core home meal planning—the stock and trade of women's "domestic" magazines—has the best intentions but typically just stresses me out. While I consider myself something of a planner, I prefer to swing like a trapeze artist through my overbooked week rather than plot out every meal.

But if you love the idea of structuring into the workweek some healthy salad meals, here's a barebones guide to customize as needed. I love restaurants and even I get tired of grocery shopping; this guide is forgiving when the last thing you want to do is spend 4 hours after work cooking. Plan a few homemade salads and suddenly you'll have time (and even a little extra money) for the important stuff (video games, long walks holding hands, knitting in a coffee shop, reading more comic books) and for eating your vegetables.

SUNDAY

Or any day you're roving around the house without a plan. That day at home you sip tea at leisure, listen to podcasts—perhaps the day laundry gets folded instead of balled up and tossed into the dresser drawer. A day you mostly go without pants.

As a general rule for making these salad elements in advance, try to use up the salad components within 5 days. For delicate lettuce and spinach leaves, eat within 2 days. For tougher kale and chopped veggies, 4 days is about their limit.

Creamy dressings are best eaten within 3 days, and vinaigrettes can go for almost a week. Tofu, tempeh, and seitan, once seasoned and cooked, should be eaten within 2 days (if it lasts that long!), but steamed, unseasoned seitan and tempeh can be wrapped up and frozen for up to 2 months!

So, here's the plan:

- Prepare and store beans for salads, such as Lentils for Salads (page 49).

- Wash, spin, and pack hearty greens such as kale or collards into produce bags, preferably the reusable "green" bags specially designed to remove ethylene gas and keep produce fresh longer than regular plastic bags. Julienne carrots, slice radishes, prepare other firm, juicy root veggies, and pop them into sealable glass containers with a little cold water.

- Bake, cool, and pack up crunchy nut toppings and croutons.

- Press tofu and seal tightly in containers. If you have the time, prepare any baked tofu toppings needed for salad recipes.

- Make a hearty salad for dinner. Make extra and pack up your lunchtime tote first before eating your fill (avoid the sog by keeping the dressing on the side to add when you're ready to eat).

MONDAY MORNING

Out the door you go, but don't forget the salad you cleverly packed up last night!

MONDAY, TUESDAY, AND WEDNESDAY

As the beginning of the week climbs up that hectic hump, stay as cool as cucumber ranch dressing with dinner salads made with a remix of those ready-to-use ingredients (beans, seasoned tofu or nuts, croutons, and greens) and fresh veggies, roasted chickpeas, or ready-to-eat proteins you prepped over the weekend. If you're making weeknight dinner salads, make a double batch of your favorite recipe; before serving yourself, pack half in a to-go container for the next day's envy-of-everyone lunch.

THURSDAY OR FRIDAY NIGHT

The workweek is (ideally) almost over, and it could be helpful to plan a few tasty bowls to start the next week right. Try planning two to three salads (one for Sunday and one or two more for early in the week) and take those first steps toward building healthful habits. If you have Friday night plans, do your shopping Thursday night!

THE WEEKEND!

Work in these helpful salad-building habits at the start of the weekend, or any morning you don't have to bolt out the door.

- Big shopping trip! Purchase produce, grains, and pantry items.

- Stock up on more green bags or containers for storing ingredients.

- Saturday afternoon or Sunday morning: make a steamy soup or fluffy pancakes. You've eaten enough salad already!

A FEW ONLINE RESOURCES

WWW.AMAZON.COM
Good old Amazon, there for your orders at 3:48 a.m. for multipacks (or monthly subscriptions) of pantry basics such as nutritional yeast, chia seeds, vinegars, chickpea flour, vital wheat gluten flour, and even unroasted cashews. Great for filling in the gaps in your kitchen equipment too (like that tofu press or a big salad spinner!).

WWW.KALUSTYANS.COM
Breathtaking selection of spices, rice, and other ethnic groceries with a focus on Indian and Middle Eastern ingredients: a handy source for za'atar, papadum, garam masala, etc.

WWW.LOCALHARVEST.ORG
Find a local farmers' market or a CSA for peak-season veggies year-round.

WWW.REUSEIT.COM
Endless options for packing your lunch salads in earth-saving, environmentally friendly style.

ROCK! THIS SALAD BOOK

In my quest for universal salad unsuckiness, I wanted to make this book really easy. And it is: you can flip to any recipe and just make it. Go ahead, ignore this section and eat something!

But, if a little advice on how to prepare your salad with grace and style, like a salad samurai, sounds good, then read on.

FIRST OFF: HOW TO USE A RECIPE

It's tempting to rip into a great-looking recipe! It's just cooking, so go for it, right? But to avoid any unexpected roadblocks, the following approach will have you flawlessly mastering any recipe:

1 Read the entire recipe.

2 Read it again, carefully this time. Make notes (mental, paper, smartphone) on what ingredients you think you need. Those ingredients that you're not 100 percent sure you have right now at home.

3 Check and see if you have all those things. Shop for what you don't.

4 Make the salad. Pay attention to anything that can save you time (chop veggies while soba noodles are cooking, etc.).

THE SPIN

Occasionally you'll see a sidebar titled "The Spin." Here you'll find helpful hints about preparing or shopping for uncommon ingredients, serving tips, or other random salad tidbits.

SAMURAI STYLINGS

Notice those swords throughout the book? These "Samurai Stylings" are suggestions on fun variations or ways to shake up the main salad recipe.

RECIPE ICONS

You'll notice two icons near each recipe title, highlighting a few points of interest:

GF **GLUTEN-FREE:** Some of these recipes contain no wheat or ingredients containing gluten. But most often, you'll see that easy gluten-free substitutions are possible (e.g., swap gluten-free soba for regular soba).

RR **RAW READY:** Recipe includes additional tips or steps to make the entire salad raw.

BASIC EQUIPMENT

Salads don't require many tools, but a few high-quality basics will make your salad days all the more pleasurable.

SALAD SPINNER

Bulky and noisy, a **salad spinner** isn't the sexiest gadget in the kitchen, but it's drop-dead gorgeous for washing and drying leafy greens, herbs, and even berries, green beans, or other small veggies. Opt for the largest salad spinner that will fit in your refrigerator and one with a lid that snaps shut to store washed salad greens.

A TONG SONG

Visit Manhattan's Midtown on a weekday during lunch and listen closely: you'll hear the clang of custom entrée salads made to order in the countless soup-and-salad chains that flourish in the ecosystem of the weekday office lunch scene. Walk in and watch a salad chef in action, and you'll see that the secret to a blazing-fast salad is using long-handled metal tongs in one hand and holding on to a big mixing bowl with the other.

Forget about those clumsy wooden salad spoons, or tossing a salad with a fork in each hand. Grab yourself a pair of thrifty, *long-handled metal tongs* and toss and serve salad like a boss.

HIGH-POWERED BLENDER

Blendtec, **Vitamix**, or even a less expensive but powerful knock-off blender will make fast work of nuts and veggies, whipping them into creamy dressings in seconds. Sure, they're pricey, but these blenders end up paying for themselves in the long run if you're a smoothie addict like me. **Old-style blenders** (the kind you need to screw off the base to clean) rarely create the smooth, creamy textures these high-powered devices offer, and most food processors can't even come close.

BIG SERVING BOWLS

In the bad old days of salad, little plates did the job of serving forgettable piles of leaves. The salads in this book are a new breed of real meals: these are bold entrées that require big bowls. Seek out shallow, **dinner-size "pasta" bowls** that can comfortably cradle at least 3 cups of real salad.

CHOP, SHRED, AND GRATE

If it takes you more than a minute to dice an average-size carrot, it may be time to reevaluate your knife and even your knife skills. A classic **chef's knife** (or a Japanese **santoku knife**) with a reasonably sharp edge will plow through vegetables faster than any food processor or the old hand-me-down kitchen knife your roommate left behind from your last move. A great knife doesn't have to cost you more than a movie and popcorn for two, and it will reward you with prepping countless fast and healthy meals. Spend a little and get a lot in return. One of my current favorite knives, a sturdy santoku knife with a solid plastic handle and a fantastic blade that destroys root veggies and tomatoes with ease, is still sharp even a year after I bought it on Amazon for less than $10.

Regarding grating and shredding, the basic **box grater** still wins. If I need only one or two carrots or beets grated for a salad, why lug out a big heavy food processor with multiple parts to clean? Within minutes a simple handheld grater can destroy vegetables. Drop this gadget into the dishwasher and you're done!

My other go-to shredder is a **Y-shaped julienne peeler**. Unlike the box grater, a Y-shaped peeler produces long, lovely noodle-like shreds of vegetables. While I opt for the box grater if I need shredded vegetables for an ingredient (such as the beet balls or carrot falafel), a Y-shaped peeler is my go-to weapon for stunning salad-worthy shreds, especially for Thai-style papaya salads.

For serious cabbage-slaying, nothing compares to a **mandoline**. Resembling a small, old-fashioned washer board but outfitted with an ultra-sharp blade, nothing turns cabbage (or beets, carrots, or any firm veg) into perfect paper-thin shreds like it. If you love safety or your fingertips, seek out models that come with added safety features.

PRESSING TOFU: A HISTORY

If there's one thing you're going to do to a block of tofu, and one thing only . . . you're just going to press it. Pressing tofu is exactly what it sounds like: apply even pressure to the tofu, remove the water, and change your attitude about this versatile, cheap vegan protein—banish watery, bland tofu forever!

Once the water is gone, tofu eagerly sucks up juicy marinades and has a firmer, toothsome texture. If you're not already using a tofu press, here is how to press it, just like your vegan grandma use to do it.

Slice 1 pound of tofu in half and slice each half again. Slice each remaining piece in half for a total of eight slabs of tofu of equal thickness. Layer a large cutting board with clean tea towels or paper towels. Arrange the tofu slices in a single layer on the towel. Spread another towel over the tofu, and then press another cutting board on top of the towel. Stack a few heavy things on the cutting board: cans, cast-iron pans, 300-page cookbooks, etc. Press tofu for 20 minutes, or up to an hour. Tofu will ooze water, so it's best to arrange this near the sink, propped on a slight angle on the edge of the sink to drain. (Or buy a tofu press and avoid tofu juice altogether!)

THE PORTABLE SALAD

Mixing everything together in a bowl is fine when it's just you, the salad, and your empty, trembling stomach. But using that big messy bowl (or eating directly out of the salad spinner—I've been there) may not be the best approach when serving guests you want to impress, or when bringing along that salad for lunch or a picnic.

LAYERED SALAD

One of my favorite ways to serve salad for nice dinner parties or just casual meals with friends is to layer the undressed ingredients on dinner plates or in bowls. Start with the fluffy greens or shredded veggies, top with more substantial fare (tempeh, beans, sliced apples, etc.), and then scatter dry toppings in a visually pleasing way. Be a salad artist! Pour the dressing into little individual serving cups and let your friends sauce up their meals.

SALAD IN A JAR

Once just the domain of food bloggers, packing salads into big wide-mouthed Mason jars is the new old thing. Glass is the ultimate salad vehicle: it keeps in the cold and keeps out weird plastic mojo, and old-timey jars give you a rustic foody pioneer vibe.

The secret to salad jar success is to pour a layer of dressing into the jar first. Then "seal" it with a layer of crunchy or firm vegetables (shredded carrot, diced radishes, roasted sweet potatoes) and lastly, top with delicate, easily wilted greens. Come time to eat, either shake the jar or dump it all into a big bowl to cover everything with tasty dressing goodness.

BENTO BOXED

The ultimate in cute! There's a colorful, shiny world of elegant multicompartment lunch boxes. Metal or plastic (BPA-free is all the rage), find one that fits your lifestyle. Start with www.reusit.com for cute lunch containers that will make you the envy of kindergarteners everywhere.

INGREDIENT TALK

Salad ingredients are old friends to most, but here's a primer on a few of the lesser-known constants in this book.

CHIA SEEDS: These tiny seeds have escaped their '80s novelty-pottery roots and are the new darling of the whole foods scene. Packed with fiber and omega-3s, they also have the unique property that when soaked in water, chia seeds create a thick gel that I use to add body (and therefore less oil) in vinaigrettes. Find organic chia seeds in natural food stores.

CHINESE 5-SPICE POWDER: A warming blend of star anise, cinnamon, fennel, cloves, and Sichuan pepper that's amazing on roasted nuts or tofu, and even in dressings. A common find in any market that has a healthy respect for good spices.

COCONUT SUGAR: A rustic sugar made from coconut palm sap, usually organic, sustainable, and vegan. It has a pronounced molasses taste: substitute with organic light brown sugar.

COCONUT WATER: The refreshing water found in the center of fresh coconuts has become insanely popular, and I love using it in vinaigrettes for its subtle texture and mellow flavor. Make sure you're using pure, unflavored, unsweetened coconut water in these recipes. And for heaven's sake don't confuse it with coconut milk (the rich creamy stuff in a can). Coconut water typically comes in paper aseptic packs similar to soy milk packaging.

GINGER, FRESH: I know what you're thinking: "Yeah, I know fresh ginger!" This is just a friendly reminder that freezing chunks of fresh ginger is effortless and prevents the sadness of discovering that lonely, dried-out lump at the bottom of the vegetable bin when you need fresh ginger the most. Scrape the skin off a big section of ginger-root with a spoon (it works great!), cut into 2-inch pieces, wrap tightly in plastic, and freeze. To use, thaw a chunk on the kitchen counter for a few minutes (partially frozen is okay), then mince or grate. Semi-frozen ginger grates up beautifully into fluffy ginger snow, perfect for whisking into dressings and marinades!

LEMONGRASS: Fresh lemongrass is simple to prepare and infuses everything with a beautiful light lemon aroma, so it's worth your time. Strip away the outer papery leaves if the stalk seems very dry and then trim off the top 6 to 7 inches (the slender, dry top of the stalk). Slice the remaining thick stem in half, then slice each half paper-thin. Or roughly dice the stem, throw it in the food processor, and pulse into a pulp. Freeze chopped lemongrass and use within 1 month. If fresh stalks aren't an option, look for chopped lemongrass in jars in gourmet or natural markets; while not as aromatic as the fresh stuff, it's the next-best thing (but avoid dried lemongrass; it's tasteless).

LIQUID SMOKE: A totally vegan seasoning liquid infused with real smoke flavor. It's intense so a little will go a long way toward infusing food with rich BBQ flavor without ever hitting the grill. Hickory and mesquite are the two most common "flavors" you'll find in any grocery store.

MÂCHE: A lovely salad green: tender, rounded little leaves with a mild sweet flavor.

MISO: Japanese fermented soybean paste, a staple of soup, that adds tons of delectable umami flavor (and saltiness) to many dressing recipes. White miso (shiro miso) is sweet, mellow, and very versatile for use in lots of recipes in this book. Bolder, richly nuanced red miso also makes an appearance.

NUTRITIONAL YEAST: A golden, flakey dried yeast powder, this vegan staple tastes so much better than it sounds. Nutritional yeast dissolves easily in liquids and has a full-bodied, robust flavor reminiscent of cheese (stinky cheese, that is). Great also sprinkled on foods, it adds a boost of rich umami flavor to plant-based cuisine along with protein and B vitamins.

PAPADUM: Savory, paper-thin Indian wafers made from ground lentils and spices. You'll find an exciting selection of flavors in Indian markets. Papadum must be cooked before eating—fried or roasted over a flame. Roasting papadum is my method of choice and is easily done on a gas range. Hold a raw papadum with long-handled metal tongs an inch or closer over a low flame until the surface bubbles and crisps, flipping and moving the papadum along the burner top until the papadum bubbles and warps to crisp perfection. You may need to practice this a few times and burn some in the process, but a few small charred spots are just fine.

PERSIAN CUCUMBERS: A small, slender variety of cucumber with a snappy texture and thin, edible skin. No peeling required! Essential for authentic Middle Eastern–style salads and so flavorful and easy to use that I prefer these instead of standard watery American cucumbers.

SALT (AS IN VERY GOOD SALT): There's table salt, and then there's really good salt. For these pure vinaigrettes, use a high-quality sea salt. For sprinkling on glazed roasted nuts or juicy slabs of August tomatoes, go hog-wild and break out the beautiful stuff like flaky Maldon, Himalayan pink, or other snobby but exceptional salts.

SRIRACHA SAUCE: Seems like all the world is in love with slathering this zingy Asian-style garlic-chile sauce over food. It's also great in marinades and fires up glazed roasted pecans, a favorite of mine in this book.

TAHINI: Creamy, pure sesame tahini is essential for so many great salad dressings. The best varieties are Middle Eastern in origin and silky smooth, but hippy organic tahini is fine too; both are usually packed in jars or tins. Don't confuse tahini with premade tahini sauce!

TAMARI: Japanese soy sauce with bold flavor and body. The darling of natural food cuisine for decades, it's usually made without added preservatives and other junk you shouldn't eat. Is gluten your archenemy? Then use gluten-free tamari!

TAMARIND CONCENTRATE: Tangy tamarind is lovely but is annoying to process by hand from fresh or dried pods. Thick brown tamarind concentrate is easy to use and adds tropical flavor to dressings and marinades. Look for it in grocery stores wherever Thai products are sold or at an Indian grocery.

TEMPEH: A firm, fermented cake of beans (usually soy) and sometimes grains like rice or barley. It's protein rich, great grilled or braised, with a delicate, nutty taste. You can find it in natural food stores, or if you're lucky at local farmers' markets (larger commercial grocery stores are starting to carry it too). In NYC, I hunt for Barry's Tempeh (www.growninbrooklyn.com).

TOFU: These recipes feature the two major types of tofu found in almost any grocery store: the grainy-textured Chinese variety and the custard-smooth Japanese type. You'll appreciate firm Chinese-style tofu for marinating and roasting, and delicate Japanese-style tofu for blending into smooth dressings.

UNROASTED CASHEWS: You may know salted, roasted cashews, but unroasted (often referred to as raw, but all cashews must be lightly cooked to remove some naturally present toxins) cashews are essential for sublime, creamy soy-free dressings. Unroasted cashews should also be unsalted. Unroasted cashews participate in many recipes in this book, so buy in bulk and store chilled.

VINEGAR: There are all kinds of vinegars! If it first can be turned into booze, it can later be made into vinegar. For this book, you'll get the most mileage from a bottle each of apple cider vinegar, red wine vinegar, and mellow rice vinegar. Ume plum vinegar, made from Japanese pickled plums, shows up in a few recipes; a little bottle of this intense fruity, salty vinegar will go a long way.

VITAL WHEAT GLUTEN FLOUR: If you're gluten-free, STOP READING HERE. The rest of you, follow me. This silky flour is the result of the starchy portion of wheat flour being removed, leaving only the pure protein of wheat (the gluten!). Grab a bag or two for making fast, easy seitan (a hearty DIY meat substitute) at home.

PART II

THE
RECIPES

DRESSED TO THRILL:
CREAMY DRESSINGS
AND SAUCY VINAIGRETTES

Oil and vinegar have a reputation for being at odds, but when forced together they make for the best and simplest of salad dressings. If you're ever stumped on how to dress a salad, remember this mantra: 1 part oil, 1 part vinegar, and a pinch of salt and pepper.

Yet woman and man cannot live only on olive oil and balsamic vinegar: creamy dressings, fruity dressings, spicy or sweet or nutty, transform ordinary produce into an inspired meal. And as complex as they are in flavor, they are easy to make.

Many of the salads in this book will have you flipping to this chapter for a luscious dressing that defines the entire entrée. What's a slaw infused with the spirit of a backyard BBQ without a smattering of ranch? Or a rustic French country salad without a splash of mustardy shallot dressing? But a few of these dressings are stand-alone wonders, "freelance" dressings not married to any salad but there for your creative salad urges. So bring your humble greens and your tofu and your chickpeas, pick a dressing, and now *you're* the salad samurai.

A helpful tip: these dressings taste best when used right away, but sometimes you need to plan and prepare ahead. Use creamy dressings within 3 days, and vinaigrettes can last as long as 7 days. Shake well before using, and, if too thick, loosen up dressings with a tablespoon of water or lemon juice.

BACK AT THE RANCH DRESSING

 GF

MAKES: ABOUT 1½ CUPS
TIME: LESS THAN 10 MINUTES, NOT INCLUDING SOAKING THE CASHEWS

Hands down, my top easy, all-around-delicious creamy salad dressing. It's ridiculously simple to transform this versatile dressing with endless herbs, spices, and condiments to garnish any salad you can imagine. Best of all, you'll never open up a jar of mayonnaise (vegan or otherwise) again, when this luscious cashew-based dressing can be made to order in minutes.

You should only make a batch when you need it, and eat within 2 days for the freshest flavor and best consistency. For everyday salads you can skip the small addition of olive oil (though it adds lovely lushness and flavor), but the addition of both garlic powder and fresh garlic adds a complexity that neither can pull off alone!

1 Soak the cashews in the hot water for 30 minutes. Then pour into a blender (including the soaking water) and blend until very smooth. Alternatively, if you have a high-powered blender (like a Vitamix or Blendtec), no soaking is required: just pulse the cashews into a fine powder, add the hot water, and pulse again until very smooth.

2 Add the remaining ingredients and pulse until smooth. Chill the dressing in a tightly covered container until ready to use, or at least 20 minutes for the flavors to blend. Store chilled and use within 2 days.

THE SPIN

There's no substitute for unroasted cashews in this recipe; unroasted nuts have a slightly sweet, dairy-like flavor. Roasted (and salted) nuts don't work as well; while tasty, they'll add a very pronounced nutty flavor and tan color that's too overpowering for this delicate, creamy ranch dressing. Whole or in pieces, look for unroasted (usually unsalted too) cashews in natural food stores, at Trader Joe's, or in large (and reasonably priced!) bags in Indian or Southeast Asian markets.

½ cup unroasted cashews

¾ cup hot water

2 tablespoons freshly squeezed lemon juice

1 tablespoon olive oil

1 clove garlic, peeled

2 teaspoons white (shiro) miso

2 teaspoons Dijon mustard

1 teaspoon garlic powder

1 teaspoon onion powder

3 tablespoons chopped fresh herbs, such as dill, basil, or tarragon

SAMURAI STYLINGS

Leave out the fresh herbs when preparing any of these variations. Often I'll make the dressing plain by default, dividing the batch in half to make two different dressings. The below additions are suggestions for full batches of dressing.

CHIPOTLE: Add 1 tablespoon minced chipotles in adobo sauce.

CURRY LIME: Add 2 teaspoons curry powder and replace the lemon juice with lime juice.

MANGO CHUTNEY: Add ¼ cup mango chutney.

RED CURRY: Add 1 to 2 tablespoons Thai red curry paste.

CREAMY SRIRACHA: Add 3 tablespoons Sriracha sauce.

MAPLE "BACON": Add 1 tablespoon maple syrup and ¼ cup of your favorite vegan bacon bits or ½ cup Coconut Bacony Bits (page 48). This dressing is best eaten as soon as it's made!

PESTO RANCH: Add 3 tablespoons prepared basil pesto.

CREAMY MAPLE MUSTARD DRESSING

½ cup unroasted cashews

½ cup hot water

¼ cup whole grain mustard

2 tablespoons maple syrup

1 tablespoon minced shallots

½ teaspoon salt

 MAKES: 1½ CUPS
TIME: LESS THAN 10 MINUTES

The rock star combination of just maple syrup and whole grain mustard makes a superb all-purpose dressing, but adding cashews adds a creamy richness that's practically illegal. It's a natural served with any of the toothsome tempeh salads in this book but is equally graceful tossed with delicate spring salad greens.

1 Soak the cashews in the hot water for 30 minutes. Then pour into a blender (including the soaking water) and blend until very smooth. Alternatively, if you have a high-powered blender (like a Vitamix or Blendtec), no soaking is required: just pulse the cashews into a fine powder, add the hot water, and pulse again until very smooth.

2 Add the remaining ingredients and pulse until creamy and smooth. Chill the dressing in a tightly covered container until ready to use, or at least 20 minutes for the flavors to blend. Store chilled and use within 2 days.

LEMON TAHINI DRESSING

GF **RR** **MAKES:** 1½ CUPS
TIME: LESS THAN 10 MINUTES

So rich and creamy, tahini-based sauces were the first foods I made when initially replacing cheese and dairy products. The dense, velvety texture of sesame tahini lends itself to endless variations of sauces, but this basic lemon tahini remains the most versatile of all.

1 In a blender, pulse all of the ingredients together until smooth. Taste the sauce and season with a dash more of salt or lemon if desired. Chill for 30 minutes; it will thicken. (If chilled overnight, it will become even thicker.) Thin out the tahini sauce by whisking in a tablespoon of cold water at a time. Store chilled and use within 2 days.

½ cup sesame tahini

¼ cup freshly squeezed lemon juice

1 clove garlic, peeled

½ teaspoon salt

⅔ cup cold water

SAMURAI STYLINGS

Pulse in the following additions:

HERBY TAHINI: **3 tablespoons chopped fresh herbs: dill, cilantro, parsley, tarragon, or a blend**

ORANGE TAHINI: **Replace the water with orange juice (freshly squeezed or store-bought) and stir in the grated zest from 1 orange.**

LEMON POPPY TAHINI: **Stir in the grated zest from 1 lemon and 1 heaping tablespoon poppy seeds.**

CHIA CHIPOTLE DRESSING

 MAKES: 1 CUP
TIME: LESS THAN 10 MINUTES

Chia seeds thicken up and add succulent, nutty body to this fruity dressing laced with smoky chipotle chiles, and it blends beautifully with Fiery Fruit & Quinoa Salad (page 97) or any grain-based salad. Sriracha lovers, take note of the easy variation with your favorite sauce!

1 Whisk together all of the ingredients in a glass or plastic measuring cup. Cover and chill for 10 minutes or overnight to plump up the chia seeds. Store chilled and use within 2 days for best flavor.

½ cup freshly squeezed or store-bought orange juice

3 tablespoons freshly squeezed lime juice

2 tablespoons olive oil

1 tablespoon chopped chipotle chiles in adobo sauce

2 teaspoons agave nectar

1 tablespoon chia seeds

1 clove garlic, minced

½ teaspoon ground cumin

½ teaspoon salt

SAMURAI STYLINGS

SRIRACHA CHIA DRESSING

Omit the chipotles in adobo sauce and substitute 2 tablespoons Sriracha sauce!

THE SPIN

Look for cans of chipotle chiles in adobo sauce where Latin American or Mexican groceries are sold. To prepare chiles for recipes, remove the chiles and save the sauce in a glass or plastic container. Mince the chiles and return them to the sauce, or to mellow their heat, slice open each chile and use the tip of a knife to scrape away the seeds before mincing. Cover tightly, keep refrigerated, and add to dressings, marinades, scrambled tofu, or beans.

ALMOND BUTTER HEMP DRESSING

 MAKES: ABOUT 1½ CUPS
TIME: LESS THAN 10 MINUTES

Nutty and loaded with heart-healthy fats, this umami-packed dressing is delicious year-round but is especially comforting on cool-weather veggies such as pumpkin, kale, or crisp shredded cabbage. Red miso is richer and bolder than white (shiro) miso and stands up to earthy almond butter. Try it as an alternate dressing on the Vanessa Kabocha Salad (page 157).

2 medjool dates

⅔ cup hot water

2 heaping tablespoons red miso

¼ cup raw almond butter

2 tablespoons hemp seeds

1 clove garlic, peeled

2 teaspoons minced fresh ginger

1 Soak the dates in the hot water for 5 minutes. Pull apart the dates and remove and discard the pits. Dump the dates and the water into a blender.

2 Add the remaining ingredients and pulse until completely smooth. Cover and chill for 10 minutes; this dressing will thicken a bit, and chilled overnight it will thicken even more. If desired, thin the dressing by whisking in a spoonful of cold water. Store chilled and use within 3 days.

 THE SPIN

Large, tender medjool dates are my favorite for adding caramel-like sweetness to nutty foods, but you can substitute 3 to 4 average-size common brown dates in this recipe.

SHALLOT MUSTARD CHIA VINAIGRETTE

½ cup pure coconut water

1 tablespoon chia seeds

2 tablespoons white wine vinegar or rice vinegar

2 tablespoons olive oil

2 tablespoons finely minced shallots (about 1 large shallot clove)

1 heaping tablespoon smooth Dijon mustard

1 tablespoon minced fresh tarragon or 1 teaspoon dried

½ teaspoon salt

¼ teaspoon freshly ground black pepper

 MAKES: ABOUT 1 CUP
TIME: LESS THAN 10 MINUTES

This is my lower-fat spin on the classic French dressing of olive oil, shallots, and mustard for a versatile vinaigrette dressing on any concoction of leafy greens, lentils, or gently blanched vegetables. The gelling properties of chia seeds and the smooth body of coconut water create a satisfying base with far less oil than the classic recipes. Because there is a little olive oil included for flavor, use top-notch cold-pressed for the most bang for your dressing buck.

1 Whisk all of the ingredients together until smooth. Pour into a glass jar, cover tightly, and chill for at least an hour to thicken slightly. Store chilled and use within 5 days for best flavor.

THE SPIN

I prefer the vinaigrette simply chilled. If you want a smooth, thick dressing, pulse in a blender until the seeds are puréed.

GALAPAGOS ISLANDS DRESSING

MAKES: 1½ CUPS
TIME: LESS THAN 10 MINUTES

I created this dressing to fill the need for that classic Thousand Island dressing, essential for the Beet Ball 'n' Fries (page 141) and Tempeh Reubenesque Salads (page 145). This creamy, savory, and sweet dressing is ready for drizzling over assertive crunchy vegetables such as cabbage, green beans, and broccoli, and great on fermented veggies like sauerkraut! Makes a great veggie dip too.

1 recipe Back at the Ranch Dressing (page 17, made without fresh herbs)

3 tablespoons all-natural ketchup

3 heaping tablespoons dill or sweet pickle relish

2 tablespoons finely minced white onion

½ teaspoon Tabasco hot sauce

1 Pulse all of the ingredients together in a blender until combined (how smooth you want it is up to you). Pour into a glass jar, cover, and chill for 10 minutes for best flavor. Store chilled and use within 2 days for best flavor.

THE SPIN No pickle relish on hand? Add ½ cup roughly chopped dill pickles and 1 teaspoon agave nectar to the ingredients and pulse as directed.

UPSTATE DRESSING

6 oil-packed sundried tomato halves, drained

½ cup warm water

¼ cup sesame tahini

3 tablespoons nutritional yeast

2 tablespoons olive oil (for more tomato flavor, use the oil from the sundried tomatoes)

2 tablespoons tamari

2 tablespoons apple cider vinegar

2 cloves garlic, peeled

GF

MAKES: ABOUT 1½ CUPS
TIME: LESS THAN 10 MINUTES

A homemade hack of Annie's Natural Woodstock Dressing, this flashback condiment can still jam with modern vegan cuisine, with its umami-rich blend of tahini, nutritional yeast, and sundried tomato. Serve this velvety dressing with leafy greens and juicy summer tomatoes. Unlike the stuff from the bottle, this dressing is uber thick and will become even thicker postrefrigeration, so you may want to thin it out by whisking in a tablespoon or two of water before serving.

1 Place all of the ingredients in a blender and pulse until perfectly smooth. Taste and season if desired with a dash more of tamari or vinegar. Cover and chill for 10 minutes before serving. Store chilled and use within 2 days. If a thinner consistency is desired, thin with 1 or 2 tablespoons of warm water before serving.

THE SPIN

Not all tahini pastes are created equal! My favorite tahini for dressings is the thinner, slicker variety typically marketed for Middle Eastern or Mediterranean cuisine (such as Roland). It's smoother, doesn't separate much, and is far easier to stir than the tahini in a can.

CREAMY CILANTRO LIME DRESSING

MAKES: ABOUT 1½ CUPS
TIME: LESS THAN 10 MINUTES

Cool, creamy lime cilantro dressing is essential for any Mexican-inspired salad or anything featuring avocado, corn, or, for a twist, fresh figs (see page 119). It's great on tacos too!

1 Soak the cashews in the hot water for 30 minutes (or overnight, refrigerated and covered). Then pour cashews and water into a blender and blend until perfectly smooth. Alternatively, if you have a high-powered blender (like a Vitamix or Blendtec), no soaking is required: just pulse the cashews into a fine powder, add the hot water, and pulse again until very smooth.

2 Add the remaining ingredients and pulse until smooth. Chill the dressing in a tightly covered container until ready to use, or at least 20 minutes for the flavors to blend. Store chilled and use within 2 days.

½ cup unroasted cashews

¾ cup hot water

2 tablespoons freshly squeezed lime juice

1 tablespoon olive oil

1 clove garlic, peeled

2 teaspoons white (shiro) miso

1 teaspoon garlic powder

1 teaspoon onion powder

1 cup lightly packed fresh cilantro

1 jalapeño pepper, roasted

THE SPIN

To roast just one pepper fast, drop it in a dry cast-iron pan preheated over high heat. Occasionally roll the pepper until nicely charred on all sides, then remove from the heat, cool for 5 minutes, and peel and discard the skin. For a milder pepper kick, remove the seeds and white inner pith before adding to the dressing.

CARROT CHIA GINGER DRESSING

 MAKES: ABOUT 1¾ CUPS
TIME: 15 MINUTES

Sweet and spicy, carrot ginger dressings look and taste great on everything. If you can make a smoothie, you can make this dressing right now! This nearly oil-free version (the minimal toasted sesame oil packs a flavor punch) gets a thickening boost from omega-3-packed chia seeds; use white seeds for maximum visual appeal, but any chia you have on hand will work in a pinch.

½ cup peeled, diced carrots

1 rounded tablespoon grated fresh ginger

2 cloves garlic, peeled

1 small white onion, chopped (about ½ cup)

2 rounded tablespoons white (shiro) miso

1 heaping tablespoon chia seeds (preferably white chia)

1 tablespoon agave nectar

¾ cup water

½ teaspoon toasted sesame oil

1 Pulse all of the ingredients together in a blender until very smooth. Pour into a glass container, seal tightly, and chill for 15 minutes or overnight; the longer the dressing chills, the thicker it gets, and the flavors blend to create a sweet, carroty mellowness. If a thinner dressing is desired, stir in a little extra water. Store chilled and use within 2 days.

SHAKE-ON SALAD CRUMBLES

GF **RR** **MAKES:** 1½ CUPS
TIME: 5 MINUTES, NOT INCLUDING DRYING AND ROASTING TIME

Inspired by the Middle Eastern nut-based dry "dip" called dukkah but with tangy, herby all-American ranch dressing flavor, this shake-on seasoning can be used to add nutty crunch and a dash of protein to salads with or without the addition of a dressing.

1 Pulse all of the ingredients in a food processor until crumbly.

2 If you have a dehydrator, spread in a thin layer on a solid dehydrator sheet and dehydrate for 6 to 8 hours until dry and crumbly. Store in a tightly covered container in the refrigerator and use within a week. If you don't have a dehydrator, spread the mixture on a baking sheet lined with parchment paper and roast at 325°F for 15 to 20 minutes. Stir occasionally and remove when the mixture starts to turn a very light golden color (don't overbrown); cool completely and store as directed.

1 cup raw, sliced almonds

¼ cup toasted or raw sesame seeds

¼ cup chopped fresh chives

2 tablespoons freshly squeezed lemon juice

1 tablespoon olive oil

1 teaspoon garlic powder

1 teaspoon onion powder

½ teaspoon salt

GREEN CURRY DRESSING

½ cup lightly packed fresh cilantro leaves

¼ cup freshly squeezed lime juice

¼ cup pure coconut water

1 jalapeño pepper, chopped (optional for a mild dressing)

2 tablespoons minced shallots

1 tablespoon mild olive oil or canola oil

1 tablespoon minced fresh ginger

1 tablespoon chopped lemongrass

1 teaspoon coconut sugar or firmly packed organic brown sugar

½ teaspoon salt

Big pinch of ground white pepper

 MAKES: ¾ CUP
TIME: LESS THAN 10 MINUTES

Do yourself a flavor favor and whip up this punchy green Thai curry-inspired dressing to liven up simple green salads, or to make the luscious Green Curry Lentil Quinoa Salad (page 88).

1 Purée all of the ingredients in a blender until as smooth as possible. Cover, chill, and use within 2 days for best flavor.

THE SPIN

Making your own curry-like dressing from scratch is really the way to go, but if you can't be bothered, whisk 3 tablespoons of store-bought green curry paste with the lime juice and coconut water. Not all curry pastes are of the same quality, so your mileage may vary!

MARVELOUS MISO DRESSING

MAKES: ABOUT 1¼ CUPS
TIME: LESS THAN 10 MINUTES

You love miso, so why not pour it all over vegetables? I put miso in many of my dressings, but this silky, versatile sauce particularly brings out the sweet 'n' mellow richness of white (shiro) miso.

1 In a mixing bowl, whisk all of the ingredients together until smooth. Cover, chill, and use within 3 days for best flavor.

½ cup white (shiro) miso

¼ cup warm water

2 tablespoons mild vegetable oil such as grapeseed oil

2 tablespoons maple syrup

1 tablespoon apple cider vinegar

½ teaspoon toasted sesame oil

AN INTERLUDE:
THE SKINNY ON SIDE SALADS

This is not a book about side salads. These are front, center, entrée salads!

However, I understand that occasionally you need one. Fair enough! I can be reasonable. Something crisp and green jazzes up a hearty entrée like nothing else (except skipping straight to dessert).

The most important ingredient for creating a simple and refreshing side salad is any ultra-fresh produce available. For me, that's from the farmers' market when possible, and in Queens, NY, that's only June through November. Be it spring arugula picked that morning or Brussels sprouts and right-off-the-tree apples in September, really fresh produce transforms into a salad with only

a shake of olive oil, a splash of lemon or vinegar, a twist of black pepper, and a pinch of good-quality salt (Himalayan pink and Maldon are favorites).

With slightly older produce that could use some help in the flavor department, I drizzle on any of the richly flavored dressings from the dressings chapter. Perhaps I'll toss in a handful of glazed nuts or seeds too.

I use the following salad "equation" for a speedy side salad that serves 2. If necessary, measure out the ingredients the first time you make it, and after that just eyeball it. Then toss everything together in a bowl and serve immediately!

SIMPLE (BUT NOT BORING) SIDE SALAD

SERVES: 2

TIME: LESS THAN 10 MINUTES

3 cups loosely packed greens (about half of a 5-ounce container)

1 to 1½ cups bite-size pieces vegetables or fruits: cherry tomatoes, green beans, cooked sweet or white potato, radishes, cucumber, blanched cauliflower, broccoli, apples, pears, berries, etc.

1 tablespoon olive oil

1 to 2 tablespoons freshly squeezed lemon juice or fruity vinegar

Salt and freshly ground black pepper to taste

1 If using a creamy dressing instead of the olive oil/lemon juice, toss the greens and veggies/fruit with about ½ cup dressing, drizzling a little extra on each serving if desired.

SIDEKICK SLAW

SERVES: 2 TO 3

TIME: LESS THAN 10 MINUTES

Simple cabbage slaw is by far my favorite companion vegetable during the winter; sweet, crisp cabbage brightens up heavy stews and heavy winter meals like a champ. With a head of green or red cabbage tightly wrapped in the fridge, I make these slaws as needed for a blast of crispy freshness, especially great alongside Latin or Caribbean dishes.

4 cups thinly sliced green or red cabbage (or a blend of both)

1 carrot, julienned, or 1 red or green apple, cored, seeded, and diced

2 tablespoons freshly squeezed lemon juice or apple cider vinegar

Salt and freshly ground black pepper to taste

2 tablespoons chopped fresh cilantro or dill (optional)

1 Combine everything in a bowl and gently massage the cabbage for a minute or two to soften it up. This slaw can be packed up, chilled, and enjoyed the next day.

RELAXED SHREDDED KALE

SERVES: 2 TO 3

TIME: LESS THAN 10 MINUTES

Is enjoying kale daily a necessity for you? This tender kale will easily fill your daily required dose of leafy green goodness.

1 pound kale (any variety)

1 tablespoon apple cider vinegar or red wine vinegar

2 teaspoons olive oil

Pinch of salt

1 If using ruffled kale, strip the leaves from the stems and tear into bite-size pieces; do this by holding onto the base of the stem with one hand, and ripping away the leaves with your other hand in one fast, swiping motion. If using lacinato (Tuscan) kale, stack the leaves and roll into tight bundles, then slice into thin ribbons.

2 Combine the kale and remaining ingredients in a mixing bowl. Massage for 1 to 2 minutes until the kale is soft and shiny. If not eating right away, store chilled in a tightly covered container and eat within a day.

SIDE SALADS

SERIOUSLY HEARTY SALAD TOPPINGS

FROM CRUNCHY TO HEARTY, THE RIGHT TOPPING TRANSFORMS A GOOD SALAD INTO SOMETHING YOU'LL DREAM ABOUT LONG AFTER THE LAST BITE.

For anyone who thinks salad is synonymous with sadness, these toppings bring a substantial protein punch to your salads: savory glazed and roasted nuts, sublimely seasoned tofu and tempeh, and hearty staples such as lentils and steamed seitan.

And then there are glorious garnishes that bring on intense cravings: garlicky, crunchy croutons, roasted hemp seed "Parmesan," and smoky, fatty-crisp coconut "bacon."

5-SPICE TAMARI ALMONDS

 **MAKES:** 1½ CUPS
TIME: 20 MINUTES

These irresistible almonds are coated with a deep mahogany glaze and fragrant with Chinese spices. A simple weeknight project, these glazed, sweet, and spicy nuts are essential in salads and for snacking too.

1 Preheat the oven to 325°F. In a 13 x 9-inch metal or ceramic baking dish, combine the almonds, agave, tamari, and 5-spice powder. Stir until the nuts are completely coated. Sprinkle with salt.

2 Roast the nuts for 16 to 18 minutes, stirring occasionally, until a sticky glaze forms. Remove from the oven and immediately transfer the nuts to a lightly oiled sheet of parchment paper or aluminum foil, and use a fork to break apart any clumps of nuts. Once completely cool, store the nuts in a tightly covered container. Use within 2 weeks.

RAW READY

Coat the nuts with the glaze, sprinkle with salt, and spread in a single layer on a solid dehydrator sheet. Dry for 8 or more hours as per manufacturer's directions.

1½ cups raw whole almonds, roughly chopped

2 tablespoons dark agave nectar

3 tablespoons tamari

2 teaspoons Chinese 5-spice powder

About ½ teaspoon coarse salt (such as Maldon)

SALAD TOPPINGS

SRIRACHA & SMOKE PECANS

1½ cups raw pecan halves

2 tablespoons maple syrup or agave nectar

1 heaping tablespoon Sriracha

½ teaspoon liquid smoke

½ teaspoon coarse salt (such as Maldon)

GF **RR** **MAKES:** 1½ CUPS
TIME: 30 MINUTES

Maple-glazed pecans kissed with piquant Sriracha and liquid smoke add a seductive crunch to any salad. They're also a must for my Collards & Sweet Potato Crunch Bowl (page 125).

1 Preheat the oven to 325°F. In a 13 x 9-inch metal or ceramic baking dish, combine the pecans, maple syrup, Sriracha, and liquid smoke. Stir until the nuts are completely coated. Sprinkle with salt.

2 Roast the nuts for 16 to 18 minutes, stirring occasionally, until a sticky glaze forms. Remove from the oven and immediately transfer the nuts to a lightly oiled sheet of parchment paper or aluminum foil, and use a fork to break apart any clumps of nuts. Once completely cool, store the nuts in a tightly covered container. Use within 2 weeks.

RAW READY

Coat the nuts with the glaze, sprinkle with salt, and spread in a single layer on a solid dehydrator sheet. Dry for 8 or more hours as per manufacturer's directions.

ROASTED HEMP SEED PARMESAN

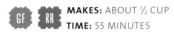 **MAKES:** ABOUT ½ CUP
TIME: 55 MINUTES

Slow-roasted hemp seeds kissed with lemon and miso create a tangy, satisfyingly fatty topping for all of the Caesar salads in this book, or simply for raining down on sliced avocado, juicy tomatoes, or even pizza!

½ cup raw, shelled hemp seeds

3 tablespoons freshly squeezed lemon juice

1 tablespoon water

2 teaspoons white (shiro) miso

1 teaspoon dried oregano

¼ teaspoon salt

1 Preheat the oven to 325°F. Pour the hemp seeds into a shallow metal or ceramic baking dish.

2 Whisk together the remaining ingredients, pour over the hemp seeds, and stir to coat the seeds in sauce. The mixture will resemble a chunky paste. Spread the seed paste in a thin layer across the bottom of the pan and roast for 15 minutes. Remove from the oven and stir with a fork to break up clumps of seeds. Return to the oven and roast for another 20 to 25 minutes.

3 Occasionally check on the seeds, stirring them around with the fork to break up the clumps. Once the marinade has been absorbed and the seeds no longer look moist, roast for a few minutes more, and use the fork to fluff the seeds until they are dry, crumbly, and golden. Remove from the oven and stir occasionally until cool. Store in a tightly covered container in the refrigerator. Use within 2 weeks.

RAW READY

Coat the seeds with marinade and spread in a single layer on a solid dehydrator sheet. Dry for 8 or more hours as per manufacturer's directions.

SALAD TOPPINGS

CURRIED CASHEW PEPITA CRUNCH

GF **RR** **MAKES:** 1½ CUPS
TIME: 30 MINUTES

1½ cups unroasted cashews

½ cup pepitas (raw, shelled pumpkin seeds)

2 tablespoons maple syrup

1 tablespoon freshly squeezed lime juice

2 teaspoons curry powder

½ teaspoon salt

Curried cashews and crunchy pumpkin seeds, with a touch of maple syrup and lime, are irresistible on salads or just eaten out of hand.

1 Preheat the oven to 325°F. In a 13 x 9-inch metal or ceramic baking dish, combine the cashews, pepitas, maple syrup, lime juice, curry powder, and salt. Stir thoroughly to coat the nuts.

2 Roast the nuts for 16 to 18 minutes, stirring occasionally, until a sticky glaze forms. Remove from the oven and immediately transfer the nuts to a lightly oiled sheet of parchment paper or aluminum foil, and use a fork to break apart any clumps of nuts. Once completely cool, store the nuts in a tightly covered container. Use within 2 weeks.

RAW READY

Coat the nuts and seeds with the glaze, sprinkle with salt, and spread in a single layer on a solid dehydrator sheet. Dry for 8 or more hours as per manufacturer's directions.

CHEEZY BUCKCRUNCH

GF **RR**

MAKES: ABOUT 3 CUPS
TIME: 30 MINUTES, NOT INCLUDING SPROUTING AND
DRYING TIME (ABOUT 2 DAYS)

After a summer of dabbling with homemade sprouted-buckwheat raw granola (all the rage, darling), I knew I wanted a savory variation for sprinkling on salads. Savor these zesty-cashewy-cheesy crumbles on hearty kale salads or on any Caesar salad.

1 About 2 days prior to making the recipe, soak, sprout, and rinse the buckwheat as directed. Pour into a large mixing bowl.

2 Cover the cashews with warm water and soak for 30 minutes. Reserve ¼ cup of the soaking liquid and drain the rest. In a blender, pulse together the cashews, the reserved liquid, and the remaining ingredients until very smooth.

3 Pour the cashew sauce over the buckwheat and stir well to coat the grains. Spread the buckwheat in a thin layer on solid dehydrator sheets and dry for 10 to 14 hours, until very dry and crisp. Store in a tightly covered container in the refrigerator. Use within 2 weeks for best flavor.

4 Alternatively, you may roast the buckwheat. The topping will have a strong toasted buckwheat flavor (similar to kasha), but hey it's still tasty! Spread the coated buckwheat on a sheet of lightly oiled parchment paper and roast at 325°F for 20 to 25 minutes, stirring occasionally, until the buckwheat is dry and lightly browned; watch carefully and don't burn! Cool completely and store as directed.

1 cup raw buckwheat, soaked and sprouted (see below)

½ cup unroasted cashews

¼ cup nutritional yeast

2 tablespoons freshly squeezed lemon juice

1 tablespoon olive oil

1 shallot, chopped

1 teaspoon onion powder

1 teaspoon sweet paprika

¾ teaspoon salt

½ teaspoon ground turmeric

SPROUT THAT BUCKWHEAT

Sprouting buckwheat is easy, but you'll need to plan ahead about 48 hours prior to making this recipe. Look for raw buckwheat groats, don't mistake them for kasha, which is roasted buckwheat with a rich reddish-tan hue. Kasha is cooked and will not sprout.

In a large mixing bowl, cover the buckwheat groats with 4 inches of cold water and soak overnight. The next morning, dump the groats into a wide colander or sieve with holes smaller than the groats and rinse well. Spread out the groats in the colander, set it on top of the mixing bowl, and allow it to rest for the next 1 to 1½ days; two to three times a day, rinse the groats with cold water.

After about 18 to 20 hours as the groats rest, you should see tiny white tails sprouting from some of the groats; leave for another 6 to 8 hours until most of the groats have sprouted. Use when the tails are about 1 centimeter.

CHIA CRUNCH CROUTONS

 MAKES: ABOUT 4½ CUPS
TIME: 45 MINUTES

½ pound good-quality, day-old crusty bread, or about 4 to 5 cups ½-inch bread cubes

⅔ cup pure coconut water

2 tablespoons chia seeds

1 tablespoon olive oil

2 tablespoons freshly squeezed lemon juice

2 cloves garlic

1 tablespoon dried herb blend (see Samurai Stylings)

½ teaspoon salt

SAMURAI STYLINGS

Use one of the following purchased or homemade herb blends for snazzier croutons.

ITALIAN HERB BLEND: purchased or homemade (oregano, rosemary, marjoram, basil)

FRENCH HERB BLEND: purchased or homemade (thyme, basil, lavender, rosemary)

ZA'ATAR

CAJUN SPICE BLEND: purchased or homemade (mix together 1 teaspoon each paprika, celery seed, thyme, garlic powder)

OLD BAY SEASONING

The gooey and omega-3-loaded goodness of chia seeds thickens a flavorful marinade for zesty, hearty homemade croutons with a fraction of the oil of traditional recipes. The most satisfying bread for rustic seeded croutons is mild, tender whole grain bread flecked with flaxseed or other seeds. Make the croutons gluten-free by using gluten-free bread.

1 If not using bread cubes, tear or cut bread into bite-size pieces or 1-inch cubes. Spread on a baking sheet lined with parchment paper and set aside to dry out, for 8 hours or overnight. Meanwhile, whisk together the remaining ingredients, cover, and chill until ready to use.

2 Preheat the oven to 350°F. Drizzle the chia seed mixture over the bread cubes and toss to coat evenly with the mixture. Bake for 30 to 35 minutes, stirring occasionally, until the bread cubes are crisp all the way through and golden. Cool completely on the baking sheet before transferring to an airtight container. Use within 1 week.

THE SPIN

Due to the high moisture and low oil content of this recipe, use only dry, firm bread cubes; fresh, soft bread will turn to mush. For the best result, cube day-old bread, spread on a baking sheet, and dry out in a warm (300°F) oven for at least 30 minutes prior to adding the marinade.

CLASSIC CROUTONS

MAKES: 4 CUPS
TIME: 45 MINUTES

Garlicky and robust old-fashioned, crunchy croutons define so many salads. A wonderful reason to recycle a day-old loaf, the flavors and textures of these croutons are only limited by the countless varieties of bread: hearty peasant loaves, crusty French, savory rye, rich whole grain loaded with seeds, nuts, and dried fruits, even dried-out cornbread! Or use your favorite gluten-free rolls or bread too.

For fun, rustic croutons, instead of cubing the bread, tear it by hand into small bite-size pieces; my favorite are made with airy ciabatta bread!

1 Preheat the oven to 350°F. Pour the bread cubes into a large mixing bowl. Whisk together the remaining ingredients in a separate bowl.

2 Drizzle a little of the dressing at a time over the cubes, stir well, drizzle more dressing, stir again, and repeat until the bread cubes are coated in dressing. Spread the cubes in a single layer on a large baking sheet (use two sheets if necessary) and bake for 25 to 30 minutes, stirring occasionally, until the cubes are completely dry and golden brown. Cool completely before transferring to loosely covered containers. Use within 7 days for best flavor.

4 cups cubed, day-old bread (about 1 pound of bread)

3 tablespoons olive oil

2 tablespoons freshly squeezed lemon juice

3 cloves garlic, minced

1 tablespoon dried herb blend or single dried herb

¼ teaspoon salt

SAMURAI STYLINGS

PITA CRISPS

Pita and similar flatbreads make great croutons too! For pita with a pocket, pull apart each pita into two halves and tear into bite-size pieces; for pocketless pita, just stack a few and slice. Prepare as directed for regular croutons.

SALAD TOPPINGS

"PICKLED" RED GRAPES

3 cups seedless red grapes

½ cup white wine vinegar or apple cider vinegar

3 tablespoons organic granulated sugar

2 teaspoons olive oil

2 teaspoons kosher salt

GF **RR**   **MAKES:** ABOUT 2½ CUPS
TIME: LESS THAN 10 MINUTES, NOT INCLUDING MARINATING

The secret's out: grapes, especially sweet and sour red grapes, are fantastic in salads. Marinate them in a simple dressing for a fast "pickled' grape to boost their sweet-sour flavor even more! Secret bonus recipe: scatter on top of a pizza right before baking, and you won't believe how great these roasted grapes can be.

1 Wash the grapes, slice each in half, and place them in a large glass container or a 2-quart glass jar. Add the remaining ingredients.

2 Screw the lid on the jar or cover with a tight-fitting lid. Shake the container vigorously for a minute and chill for 2 hours or overnight. Use within 2 days for best flavor.

THE SPIN

Roasted grapes adds delicious mystery to everything. For use in a salad, roast these pickled grapes at 400°F on a baking sheet lined with parchment paper for 6 to 8 minutes, or until the skins become slightly wrinkled and the grapes are juicy. Cool for a few minutes before adding to salads, as roasted grapes will be very hot!

MASSAGED RED ONIONS

 **GF** **RR** **MAKES:** 2 CUPS
TIME: LESS THAN 10 MINUTES

2 pounds red onions

¼ cup freshly squeezed
lime juice

1 teaspoon kosher salt

½ teaspoon organic
granulated sugar

My quest for the perfect "pickled" red onion has ended: paper-thin sliced red onions are briskly massaged with a splash of lime juice, salt, and a pinch of sugar. If raw onions are a little too much for you, you'll adore these juicy, tangy, shockingly pink onions on salads. This recipe makes a big batch that lasts for a week in the fridge, but feel free to cut the recipe in half for just enough onions for a few salads.

1 Slice off the top ½ inch of each onion (the part with the papery stem). Peel and then use a mandoline or a chef's knife to slice the onions into paper-thin shreds.

2 In a big mixing bowl, combine the onions, lime juice, salt, and sugar. Use your fingers to massage the onions until tender and bright pink, about 3 minutes. Seal in a tightly covered container and chill until ready to use. Store chilled and consume within 7 days for best flavor.

THE SPIN

One big onion about the size of a grapefruit is roughly a pound; two big onions should be perfect for this recipe. Big onions are easy to slice on a mandoline, a great (but optional) tool for creating wispy onion strands and feathery shredded cabbage too!

RED-HOT SAUCY TOFU

1 pound extra-firm tofu or super-firm tofu (no pressing necessary)

1 tablespoon refined or virgin organic coconut oil

3 tablespoons Sriracha or Frank's RedHot sauce

1 tablespoon freshly squeezed lemon juice

1 tablespoon agave nectar

SAMURAI STYLINGS

RED-HOT SAUCY TEMPEH

In place of the tofu, dice 8 ounces of tempeh into ½-inch cubes. Sauté the tempeh in the coconut oil until golden; then sprinkle with 2 tablespoons of water and sauté until the water has been absorbed. Prepare the sauce as directed, add the tempeh, and toss to coat.

TIME: a little faster, about 15 minutes!

SERVES: 2 AS A SALAD TOPPING
TIME: 30 MINUTES

You'll go bananas for these cubes of chewy pressed tofu (or tempeh!) dressed up like sautéed-and-saucy Buffalo wings. Use Frank's RedHot sauce (or your favorite vinegar-based hot sauce) for classic all-American tofu, or switch it up with Sriracha for a piquant East-West twist.

1 If using extra-firm tofu, press the tofu first (see Pressing Tofu: A History, page 9). Dice the tofu into ½-inch cubes. In a wok or cast-iron skillet, melt the coconut oil over medium heat. Add the tofu and sauté until golden on all sides, about 5 minutes.

2 In a mixing bowl, whisk together the hot sauce, lemon juice, and agave. Add the hot tofu cubes and toss them in the sauce. Serve hot or at room temperature.

THE SPIN — I prefer refined coconut oil for this dish; it has the same buttery texture of virgin coconut oil without the intense coconut flavor.

LEMONGRASS TOFU

 SERVES: 2 AS A SALAD TOPPING

TIME: 1 HOUR 15 MINUTES, MOST OF THE TIME INACTIVE, INCLUDING PRESSING AND ROASTING

Zesty lemongrass tofu is great served warm or chilled, and it adds the perfect hearty element to Asian-inspired salads like Green Papaya Salad with Lemongrass Tofu (page 79).

1 If using extra-firm tofu, press the tofu first (see Pressing Tofu: A History, page 9). Slice the tofu into thin ¼-inch strips. Preheat the oven to 400°F and coat the bottom and sides of a 13 x 9-inch ceramic or glass baking dish with cooking spray.

2 Combine the maple syrup, tamari, lemongrass, garlic, and oil in the baking dish and whisk together. Arrange the tofu slices in the marinade and set aside while the oven is preheating, about 15 minutes. Occasionally stir around the tofu strips.

3 Bake the tofu for 20 minutes. Remove from the oven and flip the strips over. Bake another 15 to 20 minutes, until the strips are golden and the marinade is absorbed. Serve warm or chilled. Store chilled and consume within 2 days for best flavor.

1 pound extra-firm tofu or super-firm tofu (no pressing necessary)

2 tablespoons maple syrup

4 teaspoons tamari

1 heaping tablespoon finely chopped fresh or prepared lemongrass

1 clove garlic, minced

2 teaspoons peanut oil or olive oil

SALAD TOPPINGS

GINGER BEER TOFU

1 pound extra-firm tofu or
super-firm tofu (no pressing
necessary)

¼ cup pure coconut water

2 tablespoons freshly squeezed
lime juice

2 tablespoons tamari

1 tablespoon light molasses

1 heaping tablespoon grated
fresh ginger

1 tablespoon olive oil

SAMURAI STYLINGS

DARK & STORMY TOFU

Add 2 tablespoons spiced rum
to the marinade.

SERVES: 2 AS A SALAD TOPPING

TIME: 1 HOUR 15 MINUTES, MOST OF THE TIME INACTIVE, INCLUDING
PRESSING AND ROASTING

**Baked tofu is bathed in a bright and gingery marinade inspired by
sunny Caribbean ginger beer. Adding a shot of rum transforms this
dish into Dark & Stormy Tofu!**

1 If using extra-firm tofu, press the tofu first (see Pressing Tofu: A History,
page 9). Slice the tofu into ½-inch strips. Preheat the oven to 400°F and
coat the bottom and sides of a 13 x 9-inch ceramic or glass baking dish
with cooking spray. Whisk together all of the ingredients except the tofu.
Add the tofu strips and flip several times to coat with marinade.

2 Bake for 30 minutes, stirring occasionally, until the marinade has been
mostly absorbed and the tofu is golden. Serve warm or chilled. Store
chilled and use within 2 days for best flavor.

3 Alternatively, you may grill the tofu on an outdoor grill or in a cast-iron
grill pan. Slice the tofu into ½-inch-thick slabs instead of strips. Oil the
pan and grill the tofu in a single layer, basting occasionally with marinade
and flipping once or twice until golden brown. Store as directed.

THE SPIN   **For true ginger beer goodness, replace the coconut
water with extra-spicy real Jamaican ginger beer!**

THAT '70S TOFU

SERVES: 2 AS A SALAD TOPPING

TIME: 1 HOUR 15 MINUTES, MOST OF THE TIME INACTIVE, INCLUDING PRESSING AND ROASTING

The humble, earthy flavors of apple cider vinegar and tamari have been seasoning tofu since the '70s, but even decades later this combo remains stylishly delicious. Sliced or cubed, it's a savory, satisfying protein that plays nicely with salads (or even sandwiches), from crowd-pleasing Caesars to pan-Asian fusion concoctions. Keep some in the fridge all weeklong for spontaneous and hearty salad creations!

1 pound extra-firm tofu or super-firm tofu (no pressing necessary)

3 tablespoons tamari

2 tablespoons apple cider vinegar

1 tablespoon olive oil

1 clove garlic, minced

½ teaspoon sweet paprika

1 If using extra-firm tofu, press the tofu first (see Pressing Tofu: A History, page 9). Slice the tofu into ½-inch strips. Preheat the oven to 400°F and coat the bottom and sides of a 13 x 9-inch ceramic or glass baking dish with cooking spray. Whisk together all of the ingredients except the tofu. Stir in the tofu strips to coat with marinade and set aside while the oven preheats, about 20 minutes. Flip the tofu once after about 10 minutes.

2 Bake the tofu for 30 minutes. Remove from the oven, flip the tofu over once more, and bake another 5 to 10 minutes, until golden and the marinade has been absorbed. Serve warm or chilled. Store chilled and use within a week.

SALAD TOPPINGS

MAPLE ORANGE TEMPEH NIBBLES

8 ounces tempeh

½ cup freshly squeezed or
store-bought orange juice

2 tablespoons soy sauce

2 tablespoons pure maple syrup

1 teaspoon Sriracha

1 tablespoon peanut oil
or olive oil

MAKES: ABOUT 1½ CUPS
TIME: 30 MINUTES

**Savor these citrusy bites of toothsome tempeh while still warm on top
of any leafy salad! They're also remarkably tasty served on the shredded beets and seaweed in Mermaid's Picnic Salad with Seahorse Ranch
Dressing (page 95) or with Fresh Fig & Tempeh Salad with Creamy
Cilantro Lime Dressing (page 119).**

1 Dice the tempeh into ½-inch cubes. In a small bowl whisk together the
orange juice, soy sauce, maple syrup, and Sriracha.

2 Heat the oil in a 10-inch cast-iron skillet over medium heat. Add the
tempeh and spread into a single layer in the pan. Fry for 3 minutes,
occasionally flipping the cubes with a spatula to brown all the sides. Pour
the marinade over the tempeh and simmer for 4 to 6 minutes, stirring
occasionally, until the marinade has been absorbed and the cubes are
coated in a rich glaze. Use the spatula to transfer the tempeh to a plate.
Scatter the cubes over salads warm or at room temperature. Store chilled
and consume within 2 days for best flavor.

TEMPEH BACON BITES

MAKES: ABOUT 1½ CUPS
TIME: 20 MINUTES

Bacon-flavored tempeh is an essential recipe that no modern vegan chef should be without. This no-fuss recipe relies on pantry staples and yields sweet 'n' smoky, bite-size pieces that romance any spinach salad, or, when prepared as strips, is the soul of my favorite winter salad: Tempeh Reubenesque Salad (page 145).

1 Slice the tempeh into ¼-inch-thin strips. Then stack a few strips at a time and slice the tempeh into bite-size pieces, about 1 inch long.

2 In a ceramic or metal baking dish, whisk together the remaining ingredients until smooth. Add the tempeh bits and gently toss to completely coat with marinade. Let stand for 10 minutes or cover and chill overnight.

3 Use a fork to transfer the tempeh pieces (leaving the marinade behind) to a lightly oiled cast-iron skillet preheated over medium heat. Lay the pieces in a single layer, and if desired spritz with a little cooking spray. Cook until well browned on one side, flip, and cook the other side until browned, about 2 to 3 minutes per side. After the tempeh is browned on both sides, pour the marinade over it and simmer until the marinade is absorbed. Serve hot, warm, or at room temperature. Store chilled and consume within 2 days for best flavor.

8 ounces tempeh

2 tablespoons pure maple syrup

2 tablespoons tamari

1 tablespoon all-natural ketchup

1 tablespoon vegetable oil

¾ teaspoon liquid smoke

Olive oil, for pan-frying

THE SPIN

As mentioned, slice the tempeh into bite-size pieces for a tossed salad. If serving in a hearty layered salad, consider leaving the tempeh in strips for maximum visual effect!

SALAD TOPPINGS

COCONUT BACONY BITS

GF **RR**   **MAKES:** 2 CUPS
                   TIME: 30 MINUTES

2 tablespoons tomato paste

2 tablespoons pure maple syrup

4 teaspoons liquid aminos
(such as Bragg's or coconut
liquid aminos) or tamari

1 tablespoon liquid smoke
(preferably hickory)

2 heaping cups large,
unsweetened coconut flakes

Bacon-flavored crunchy coconut chips? Hell yes, and you know you want some! And so easy to make too. You'll go bonkers for these sweetly smoky, big flakes of roasted coconut not just on salads, but on steamed veggies and pasta—even scattered on granola for breakfast. Great prepared totally raw in a dehydrator too!

A note about liquid aminos: I like the old-school vegan flavor of Bragg's in this recipe, but you can substitute coconut aminos or even tamari. If you've never seen a bottle of Bragg's liquid aminos before, any natural food store will have some.

1 Preheat the oven to 325°F and line a large baking sheet with parchment paper.

2 In a large mixing bowl, whisk the tomato paste, maple syrup, liquid aminos, and liquid smoke until smooth. Pour in the coconut flakes and use a rubber spatula to thoroughly stir together, completely coating the flakes with the marinade.

3 Spread the flakes in a thin layer on the parchment paper and roast for 15 to 20 to minutes, stirring occasionally, until the flakes are completely dry and slightly glossy. Cool completely before packing in an airtight container and store in a dark, cool place. Consume within 2 weeks for best flavor.

RAW READY

Coat the flakes with the marinade and spread them in a single layer on a solid dehydrator sheet. Dry for 8 or more hours as per manufacturer's directions.

THE SPIN

Seek out big, unsweetened coconut flakes instead of shredded or grated coconut for this recipe. Bob's Red Mill carries a wonderful flaked coconut (www.bobsredmill.com/coconut-flakes.html), or investigate Indian markets for dried, flaked coconut.

LENTILS FOR SALADS

MAKES: 3 CUPS
TIME: 50 MINUTES

1 cup firm-textured uncooked lentils (such as black, brown, or French)

2¼ cups water

2 bay leaves

½ teaspoon dried thyme

½ teaspoon salt

Lightly seasoned lentils are a satisfying topping or main ingredient in entrée salads. You can and should try cooking other beans from scratch too (such as black beans and chickpeas), but unlike other beans, lentils require no soaking and cook quickly, making them an easy veggie protein. Freeze half the batch in plastic bags for lentils anytime, any salad.

1 Pick over the raw lentils to remove any debris or anything nonlentily. Pour into a fine-mesh sieve, rinse, and transfer to a large saucepan.

2 Add to the saucepan the water, bay leaves, thyme, and salt and bring to a rolling boil over high heat for 3 minutes. Turn down the heat to low, cover, and cook for 40 to 45 minutes, or until almost all of the water has been absorbed and the lentils are tender. Turn off the heat, uncover, and gently stir with a fork. Cool for 20 minutes or chill before using. Store chilled and consume within 4 days for best flavor.

STEAMED OR BAKED SEITAN CUTLETS

MAKES: 4 PORTIONS OF SEITAN
TIME: ABOUT 45 MINUTES

1½ cups cold, richly flavored vegetable broth

2 cloves garlic, minced or grated with a microplane grater

3 tablespoons soy sauce or liquid aminos (such as Bragg's)

2 tablespoons olive oil

1¾ cups vital wheat gluten flour (one 10-ounce package)

¼ cup nutritional yeast

¼ cup chickpea flour

½ teaspoon ground cumin

Seitan, that clever "meat from wheat" still ushers in questions from newbies: what is it, what do you do with it, and how do you pronounce it? Let it be a mystery no longer! If you can knead dough, you can make say-tan (and it's easier than making bread).

These rustic cutlets are the easiest version of the ultra-simple steamed seitan I've been making for years, but you can also bake them for a dense, chewy texture. Either way, just mix, wrap, and cook for a succulent, handmade veggie protein that loves marinades and is great on the grill for a "meaty" salad topping. Note: I've provided the option of grating the garlic with a microplane grater; if you prefer your garlic flavor evenly distributed throughout the seitan (rather than tasting flecks of garlic), please try this method!

1 In a 1-quart glass measuring cup or bowl, whisk together the vegetable broth, garlic, soy sauce, and olive oil. In a separate bowl, stir together the vital wheat gluten flour, nutritional yeast, chickpea flour, and cumin. Form a well in the center and pour in the broth mixture.

2 Stir with a rubber spatula; when all of the broth has been absorbed and the dough pulls away from the sides of the bowl, use both hands and knead the dough for a minute. For the best texture results, knead the dough in one direction, using a folding and pressing motion with your palms. Let the dough rest for 10 minutes and then slice it into four equal pieces.

3 Tear off four 10-inch-long pieces of aluminum foil. In the center of each piece of foil, pat each piece of dough into a thin oval less than ½ inch thick. Now seal each packet for steaming: bring the long edges of the foil together and fold together with a seam about ¼ inch wide, then fold another seam, and press together to tightly seal; there should be some space between this little foil tent and the seitan inside. Tightly crimp the opposite ends; the result should be a loose foil pouch with tightly sealed seams. The seitan will expand as it steams, so make sure you have some room left over in the foil pouch! Repeat with the remaining seitan portions.

4 Set up your steamer and steam the seitan for 25 minutes. Take care that the seitan does not touch the water. The loaves will expand and feel firm when done; if not, continue to steam for another 5 minutes. Remove the seitan from the steamer, don't unwrap yet, and cool on the kitchen counter for 20 minutes before using. For best flavor and texture, cool the seitan to room temperature, then chill overnight. Store chilled in a tightly covered container and consume within 7 days for best flavor. If desired, wrap and freeze the seitan and use within 2 months; to defrost, leave it in the refrigerator overnight.

5 Alternatively, you can bake the seitan in a preheated 350°F oven for 30 minutes. Make sure to leave room in the foil pouches even if you're baking the seitan; it will expand during baking too! Cool and store as directed.

THe SPIN

This seitan is modestly seasoned and designed to harmonize with marinades and zesty dressings. For a flavored seitan, stir into the liquid ingredients 1 to 2 teaspoons of tomato paste or dried herbs such as thyme, oregano, or any blend.

Chickpea flour makes an appearance here; this dense, golden flour is made from ground chickpeas and adds rich umami flavor to seitan. Find it in natural food stores, or wherever gluten-free baking ingredients are sold.

SPRING

EARLY SPRING MAY HAVE THE SLIMMEST PICKINGS WHEN IT COMES TO FRESH GREEN PRODUCE, BUT IT'S ALSO WHEN WE NEED IT THE MOST.

By the end of winter, everyone is tired of pasta and potatoes, and ready for the crisp, leafy textures and cooling, bitter flavors of spring veggies. These are vibrant salads bursting with tender new greens and bright herbs, but they are built upon a hefty foundation of pantry staples and year-round tropical favorites.

SPRING HERB SALAD WITH MAPLE ORANGE TEMPEH NIBBLES

SERVES: 2 TO 3

TIME: 20 MINUTES, NOT INCLUDING MAKING THE TEMPEH OR PECANS

Taste a little springtime in each bite: bright strawberries, crunchy toasted pecans, and tender baby greens. Radishes too: seek out mellow finger-shaped French breakfast radishes for all their sweetness, without the bitter heat of globe radishes. It's a whole farmers' market in a salad bowl, and a protein-packed treat when topped with nuggets of orange-glazed tempeh.

1 Whisk the dressing ingredients together in a glass measuring cup or bowl. Use a salad spinner to wash and dry the greens and herbs and then place them in a large mixing bowl. Slice the strawberries ¼ inch thick and add to the salad along with the scallions, radishes, and snap peas.

2 Add the tempeh and pecans to the salad and pour on the dressing. Use long-handled tongs to toss the salad, gently grabbing the ingredients but thoroughly coating each salad element with dressing. Serve it!

THE SPIN

Busy chefs should prep the following up to a day in advance: chill the marinated tempeh, roast the pecans, make the dressing, and store it all separately. Prep the salad veggies/fruits up to 8 hours before: clean and dry the greens, herbs, strawberries, scallions, radishes, and snap peas and chill in a large sealed plastic bag. Just prior to serving, cook the tempeh, slice the strawberries, and serve!

DRESSING

1 small shallot, minced

2 tablespoons olive oil

2 tablespoons freshly squeezed lemon juice

1 tablespoon agave nectar

Grated zest of 1 lemon

½ teaspoon salt

Freshly ground black pepper to taste

SPRING HERB SALAD

5 cups baby arugula or a blend of baby salad greens

1 cup flat-leaf parsley (stems removed)

½ cup fresh dill or basil leaves, roughly chopped

1 pint strawberries, hulled, washed, and patted dry

4 scallions, green part only, very thinly sliced on a diagonal

1 cup thinly sliced mild radishes

1 cup snap peas, very thinly sliced on a diagonal

SALAD TOPPINGS

1 recipe Maple Orange Tempeh Nibbles (page 46)

1 cup Sriracha & Smoke Pecans (page 34) or toasted pecans

DEVILED KALE CAESAR SALAD

SERVES: 2 TO 3
TIME: 45 MINUTES

Dig into this fabulously spicy twist on kale Caesar salad, devilishly dressed in a piquant and creamy paprika and roasted red pepper dressing. It's bursting with plenty of smoked paprika for an alluring bite and Russian red kale and Massaged Red Onions (page 41) for a dramatic rosy entrée. Classic croutons are welcome here, or go bold and use broken shards of crispy flatbread crackers.

1 Soak the cashews in the hot water for 30 minutes, until tender. Pulse the cashews and soaking water in a blender along with the roasted red pepper, sweet paprika, hot paprika, lemon juice, olive oil, garlic, miso, and mustard. Cover and chill the dressing for 10 minutes or overnight.

2 When ready to serve, toss the dressing with the kale and croutons in a large bowl until completely coated. Transfer to serving plates and garnish with the pickled onions, if desired, and a dusting of paprika.

DEVILED CAESAR DRESSING

½ cup unroasted cashews

½ cup hot water

1 roasted red pepper (store-bought or homemade), seeded

2 teaspoons sweet paprika

½ teaspoon hot paprika or cayenne pepper to taste

2 tablespoons freshly squeezed lemon juice

1 tablespoon olive oil

3 cloves garlic, peeled

2 teaspoons white (shiro) miso

1 tablespoon Dijon mustard

KALE SALAD

6 cups curly or Russian red kale, washed and torn into bite-size pieces

1 recipe Classic Croutons (page 39), made with pumpernickel bread, or 6 ounces crisp flatbread crackers broken into bite-size shards

½ cup Massaged Red Onions (page 41, optional) plus sweet paprika, for garnish

STRAWBERRY SPINACH SALAD WITH ORANGE POPPY SEED DRESSING

 SERVES: 3 TO 4
TIME: 50 MINUTES

Berries always find their way into my favorite spring salads, but strawberries and blueberries are the centerpiece of this gorgeous salad. Frozen orange juice concentrate packs zesty flavor into the sunny poppy seed dressing, which also doubles as a marinade for the chewy, baked tofu.

1 Press the tofu (see Pressing Tofu: A History, page 9). Meanwhile, whisk the dressing ingredients together in a bowl. Slice each piece of tofu into four rectangles and then slice each rectangle into two triangles. When you're done, you'll have a bunch of little tofu triangles!

2 Preheat the oven to 400°F and lightly oil a 9 x 13-inch ceramic baking dish. Lay the tofu triangles in the pan, pour half of the dressing over the tofu, and bake for 10 minutes. Remove from the oven, flip each piece over, and brush with the marinade from the bottom of the dish. Return to the oven and bake another 15 to 20 minutes, or until the tofu is golden. Set aside to cool while you prepare the rest of the salad.

3 Wash, spin dry, and tear the spinach into bite-size pieces. Transfer to a big serving bowl and add the fruit, onions, pecans, and tofu triangles. Pour on the remaining dressing and toss well. Summon your salad-loving cohorts and eat!

 **THE SPIN**

The dressing can be made and stored in the fridge up to 4 days in advance, along with the tofu. Store washed, spun-dry greens in a green bag for up to a week.

ORANGE POPPY SEED DRESSING AND TOFU

1 pound extra-firm tofu

½ cup orange juice concentrate, thawed

¼ cup olive oil or grapeseed oil

¼ cup minced shallots

2 tablespoons freshly squeezed lemon juice

2 tablespoons agave nectar or pure maple syrup

1 tablespoon Dijon mustard

1 tablespoon poppy seeds

¾ teaspoon sea salt

½ teaspoon freshly ground black pepper

SPINACH SALAD

6 cups fresh spinach (or other salad greens, such as baby mixed greens, arugula, red leaf lettuce, Boston lettuce, butter lettuce)

2 cups sliced strawberries

1 cup blueberries

1 large red onion, sliced into thin half-moons

1 cup Sriracha & Smoke Pecans (page 34)

BLUEBERRY TAMARI GREENS BOWL

SERVES: 2
TIME: 10 MINUTES

This unexpectedly delicious combination of blueberries, cucumbers, and savory tamari dressing is habit forming. Served on spinach it is dandy, but if you can find delicate tatsoi (a Japanese green akin to tender bok choy) use that instead!

1 Place the blueberries, cucumbers, scallions, and greens in a large salad bowl. In a glass measuring cup or bowl, whisk together the tamari, maple syrup, sesame oil, sesame seeds, ginger, and red pepper.

2 Pour the dressing over the salad, toss to coat, and divide among serving bowls. Top with almonds and tofu, if using, and serve.

THE SPIN Look for the shichimi red pepper blend in little glass jars in Asian markets.

1 pint blueberries

3 Persian cucumbers, diced into ½-inch cubes

2 scallions, green parts only, thinly sliced

4 cups baby spinach or tatsoi leaves, torn into bite-size pieces, washed, and spun dry

3 tablespoons tamari

1 tablespoon pure maple syrup

2 teaspoons toasted sesame oil

1 tablespoon toasted sesame seeds

1 teaspoon grated fresh ginger

½ teaspoon red pepper flakes or Japanese red pepper blend (shichimi)

1 cup 5-Spice Tamari Almonds (page 33)

Ginger Beer Tofu (page 44) or Lemongrass Tofu (page 43), chopped into 1-inch cubes (optional)

TEMPTING TATSOI

I originally developed this recipe using this uncommon Japanese salad green instead of spinach, which unlike tatsoi is widely available year round. Similar in appearance to a smaller, slender bok choy with tender, sweet leaves, tatsoi adds a special touch to this Asian-inspired dish. Tatsoi has a very brief season: late spring through early summer.

GRILLED KALE SALAD
WITH SPICY LENTILS

SERVES: 2

TIME: 30 MINUTES, NOT INCLUDING COOKING THE LENTILS

Grilled kale marinated with coconut milk pairs wonderfully with lentils: the kale grills in a flash, so it's easy to fire up a cast-iron grill pan on the stove for flavor that rivals grilling in the great outside. Enjoy this salad year-round, or in the early spring (or late fall) when lacinato (Tuscan) kale is at its sweetest after a touch of frost.

1 Trim away the tough bottom inch from each stem of kale and discard. Slice the stems into 3-inch-long sections. Transfer to a bowl and add the scallions. Pour in the coconut milk and lime juice, add a pinch of salt, and massage the kale and scallions just enough to coat them with dressing. Preheat a cast-iron grill pan over high heat.

2 Remove only the kale from the bowl and grill it for about 30 to 45 seconds, flipping once, until it is tender and perhaps slightly charred. Transfer to a dish. Grill the scallions for about 1 to 2 minutes, transfer to a cutting board, and slice into bite-size pieces when just cool enough to handle.

3 In the bowl with the leftover coconut lime dressing, whisk in the vinegar and Sriracha. Add the lentils, onion, tomatoes, and almonds and toss to coat with the dressing. Mound the lentil mixture in individual serving dishes, arrange the kale and scallions on top, and serve with lime wedges.

1 pound lacinato (Tuscan) kale

1 bunch (about 6) scallions, root ends trimmed

1 cup coconut milk (full fat or reduced fat)

2 tablespoons freshly squeezed lime juice

Pinch of salt

1 tablespoon red wine vinegar

2 tablespoons Sriracha

1½ cups Lentils for Salads (page 49) or cooked canned lentils, drained and rinsed

1 red onion, diced

1 pint cherry or grape tomatoes, sliced in half

¼ cup toasted, chopped almonds

Lime wedges, for garnish

THE SPIN

The coconut lime marinade doubles as a dressing in this salad, but if you require a little extra something to drizzle on the finished dish, serve it with Sriracha Chia Dressing (page 20).

ASPARAGUS PAD THAI SALAD

SERVES: 2
TIME: 45 MINUTES

Put down that wok and pick up a veggie peeler for this fusion of raw culinary technique (shredding asparagus or zucchini into "noodles"), cooked rice noodles, and a dressing of caramelized shallots for a lighter, veggie-loaded twist on that beloved Thai noodle dish.

1 Boil the rice noodles according to package directions and cook only until al dente (1 or 2 minutes less than directed). Drain, rinse with cold water, and cover with cold water until ready to use.

2 Wash and trim the tough stem ends from the asparagus. Trim the heads from the asparagus and set aside. Use a Y-shaped peeler to shred the asparagus stalks into long ribbons and slice into thin strips the remaining pieces that are too awkward to shred. Transfer the asparagus ribbons to a mixing bowl and add the mung bean sprouts, basil, cilantro, and scallions.

3 In a skillet over medium heat, fry the shallots, garlic, ginger, and oil until the shallots are golden brown, about 3 minutes. Add the asparagus tips, sauté 1 minute, remove from the heat, and cool for 2 minutes. Transfer the asparagus tip mixture to the bowl with the ribbons. Drain the rice noodles and add to the asparagus salad.

4 Whisk together the lime juice, sugar, tamarind, and soy sauce and pour over the salad. Toss to coat everything with dressing. Mound the salad in serving bowls and garnish with strips of Lemongrass Tofu and sprinkle with peanuts. Devour, but graciously offer wedges of lime, Sriracha, a small dish of coconut sugar, and soy sauce for dining companions to season their own dish to taste.

THE SPIN Plan ahead like a samurai: prepare the Lemongrass Tofu a day in advance and heat up just before serving.

PAD THAI SALAD

4 ounces Pad Thai rice noodles

½ pound asparagus

1 cup mung bean sprouts, washed and dried

1 cup lightly packed fresh Thai or sweet basil leaves, chiffonaded

1 cup lightly packed fresh cilantro, coarsely chopped

2 scallions, green part only, thinly sliced

1 recipe Lemongrass Tofu (page 43)

½ cup roasted peanuts, coarsely ground

Lime wedges and Sriracha, for serving

TOASTED SHALLOT DRESSING

¼ cup minced shallots

2 cloves garlic, minced

1 tablespoon minced fresh ginger

1 tablespoon vegetable oil

¼ cup freshly squeezed lime juice

2 tablespoons coconut sugar or organic brown sugar, plus more for serving

1 tablespoon tamarind concentrate

1 tablespoon soy sauce, plus more for serving

SAMURAI STYLINGS

ZUCCHINI NOODLE PAD THAI

Replace the rice noodles with homemade zucchini or yellow summer squash noodles for an even lighter dish. You'll need a little more than ½ pound of squash. Use the Y-shaped peeler to create long, thin strands similar to the asparagus "noodles" for the above salad. Proceed as directed.

SPRING

THAI SEITAN LARB IN LETTUCE CUPS

SERVES: 3 TO 4
TIME: 45 MINUTES

A wonderful contrast of hot and cold, spicy and crunchy, this seitan version of a traditional Thai dish of spicy minced meat and veggies tucked into large edible leaves (or lettuce) is lovely to behold and fun to eat. Gluten-free? Then opt for the even faster and hearty lentil variation!

1 In a food processor, pulse together the shallots, lemongrass, lime, chiles, garlic, ginger, soy sauce, and salt. In a large skillet, heat the oil over medium heat and add the pulsed mixture. Sauté for 3 to 4 minutes, until the shallots are translucent. Meanwhile, chop the seitan in the food processor. Add the seitan to the skillet and continue to fry for another 4 minutes, or until seitan is heated through. If the seitan starts to stick, deglaze the pan with a few tablespoons of water or vegetable broth.

2 Make the dressing: whisk together all of the dressing ingredients in a small bowl and set aside until ready to serve.

3 Serve the larb! Scoop the hot seitan larb into lettuce leaves and arrange on a serving dish. Or for a nontraditional, casual meal, pile it on top of salad greens arranged in serving bowls. Drizzle with a little dressing, garnish with cilantro and curried cashews, and eat immediately, passing around any leftover dressing.

THE SPIN

Look for fresh or frozen whole kaffir lime leaves where Southeast Asian produce is sold, or substitute 1 teaspoon unpacked grated lime zest in place of the leaves. To prepare fresh lemongrass, see the lemongrass entry in Ingredient Talk (page 11). You can use regular soy sauce or tamari, but mellow Thai soy sauce tastes rich and nuanced here. Look for Thai soy sauce and fiery little red Thai chiles in Thai grocery stores.

SEITAN LARB

¾ cup coarsely chopped shallots

2 tablespoons thinly sliced lemongrass

3 kaffir lime leaves, thinly sliced, or 1 teaspoon unpacked grated lime zest

1 to 3 small red Thai chiles, seeded and chopped

2 cloves garlic, minced

1 tablespoon minced fresh ginger

2 teaspoons Thai light soy sauce or regular soy sauce

½ teaspoon salt

3 tablespoons peanut oil or mild vegetable oil

2 Steamed Seitan Cutlets (page 50), roughly diced

10 or more large, crisp lettuce leaves, hearts of romaine leaves, or 4 to 6 cups of mixed spring greens

CHILE LIME DRESSING

⅓ cup freshly squeezed lime juice

2 tablespoons Thai light soy sauce or regular soy sauce

2 rounded tablespoons coconut sugar or organic brown sugar

2 teaspoons Sriracha

GARNISH

1 cup lightly packed cilantro sprigs

½ cup Curried Cashew Pepita Crunch (page 36) or roasted, chopped peanuts

SAMURAI STYLINGS

LENTIL LARB

Substitute the seitan with 2 cups of Lentils for Salads (page 49) or cooked canned lentils. Firm black or French lentils work best.

LENTIL PÂTÉ BANH MI SALAD ROLLS

MAKES: 10 OR MORE ROLLS
TIME: 1 HOUR

A dollop of homemade lentil walnut pâté adds French flair to these piquant salad rolls inspired by Vietnamese banh mi sandwiches. The essentials of a banh mi sandwich—cilantro, daikon (or as in the photo, watermelon radish), carrot, and a creamy veggie pâté—are all here, along with a crunchy surprise: a single cornichon pickle.

1 Make the pâté first: in a skillet, sauté the shallots in oil until golden. Then add the garlic and ginger and sauté for 1 minute. Stir in the sherry, simmer for 30 seconds, and then add the thyme, mustard, and nutmeg. Turn off the heat and cool for 5 minutes.

2 In a food processor, pulse the toasted walnuts into a meal as fine as possible. Add the lentils and sautéed shallots and pulse into a thick paste, stopping occasionally to scrape down the sides and bottom of the processor bowl. Add the vinegar, salt, and black pepper. Pulse again, then taste and, if necessary, season with another dash of vinegar or salt. Spoon the lentil paste into a mixing bowl, cover with plastic wrap, and refrigerate until completely chilled, at least 1 hour or overnight.

3 When ready to assemble the rolls, prepare all of the salad vegetables first, then whisk together the sauce ingredients and pour into small condiment dishes. Fill a wide, shallow bowl with 1 inch of warm water for reconstituting the rice paper.

4 Get ready to roll! Soften a rice paper wrapper by submerging it in the water dish for about 15 seconds, or until it's softened just enough to bend; do not oversoak or the wrappers will easily tear. Gently shake away any excess water and spread the wrapper on a cutting board.

BLACK LENTIL PÂTÉ

¼ cup chopped shallots

1 tablespoon peanut oil or coconut oil

1 tablespoon chopped garlic

1 teaspoon chopped fresh ginger

3 tablespoons cooking sherry

1 teaspoon dried thyme

1 teaspoon Dijon mustard

½ teaspoon ground nutmeg

1 cup toasted, chopped walnuts

1 (15-ounce) can cooked black lentils, drained and rinsed

½ teaspoon balsamic vinegar or Chinese black vinegar

¼ teaspoon sea salt or to taste

Few twists freshly ground black pepper

SALAD ROLLS

2 cups shredded romaine lettuce

1 cup cucumber matchsticks

½ cup carrot matchsticks

½ cup radish or daikon matchsticks

1 cup cilantro sprigs (use tender stems with leaves)

10 scallion stems (green part only)

10 or more cornichon pickles

10 or more 8-inch rice paper wrappers

(continued)

SPRING

3 tablespoons soy sauce

1 tablespoon rice vinegar

1 tablespoon finely chopped fresh chives

½ teaspoon Dijon mustard

5 Arrange on the lower third of the wrapper a few tablespoons of the shredded lettuce, a few strands of cucumber, carrot, and radish, a sprig of cilantro, and a scallion stem. Scoop up about 2 tablespoons of pâté and work into an oblong shape. Press it onto the lettuce and then gently press a cornichon into the pâté. Gently fold the sides of the wrapper over the filling, then roll up the wrapper, bottom to top, like a burrito. Serve along with the dipping sauce!

6 Rolls are best consumed within 30 minutes of assembling, but if packed in an airtight, dry container and chilled, they can be enjoyed a few hours later.

THE SPIN

Round rice paper wrappers, also called salad roll wrappers or rice paper spring roll wrappers, are common enough in Asian markets and many gourmet and natural food stores that it's easy to find them in many sizes. Look for large wrappers at least 8 inches wide and up to 10 inches. Chinese black vinegar can be found in most Asian markets, but affordably priced balsamic vinegar makes a decent substitute.

SEARED GARLIC CHICKPEAS, SPINACH & FARRO

SERVES: 2 TO 3
TIME: 30 MINUTES

My favorite mix of Spanish flavors—capers, olives, raisins, and sherry vinegar—tangled with chewy farro, spinach, and chickpeas seared with garlic is a lovely transition from chilly spring to warmer days ahead. If you just happen to have a ripe avocado, throw it in for additional buttery richness.

1 In a large salad bowl, combine the farro, spinach, raisins, pine nuts, and olives. Whisk together the dressing ingredients in a small bowl.

2 In a large skillet, heat the olive oil over medium heat, add the garlic, and fry for 30 seconds. Increase the heat to high and add the chickpeas and capers. Fry the chickpeas for 3 to 4 minutes, until browned and seared on the surface. Turn off the heat and toss with the lemon juice, salt, and pepper.

3 Transfer the hot chickpeas to the salad, add the dressing, and use tongs to combine and coat everything with dressing. Serve immediately.

 THE SPIN

Cooked whole grains stand up to the assertive flavors in this salad. For gluten-free options try cooked whole oat groats or quinoa.

COOKING FARRO

Pick through and rinse 1 cup farro and combine in a saucepan with 5 cups of water and a pinch of salt. Bring to a boil for 5 minutes, reduce the heat, and simmer for about 20 minutes, until tender. Drain and set aside to cool while preparing the other salad ingredients, or cook the night before and chill until ready to use.

SALAD

1 cup cooked farro (prepared per package directions), slightly warm or cooled to room temperature

6 cups baby spinach (5-ounce package)

½ cup dark raisins

⅓ cup toasted pine nuts or slivered almonds

¼ cup pitted, sliced Kalamata olives

DRESSING

3 tablespoons olive oil

¼ cup minced shallots

2 tablespoons sherry vinegar

1 tablespoon pure maple syrup

1 teaspoon Dijon mustard

1 teaspoon dried thyme

½ teaspoon smoked sweet paprika

½ teaspoon salt

SEARED GARLIC CHICKPEAS

1 tablespoon olive oil

4 cloves garlic, minced

1 (14-ounce) can chickpeas, drained and rinsed

2 tablespoons capers

1 tablespoon freshly squeezed lemon juice

¼ teaspoon salt

Few twists freshly ground black pepper

COUSCOUS WITH SNAP PEAS & ZA'ATAR DRESSING

COUSCOUS SALAD

1 cup uncooked Israeli couscous (preferably whole wheat)

1½ cups water

½ teaspoon salt

4 large dried figs, diced into bite-size pieces

1 cup thinly sliced radishes

½ pound snap peas, sliced on the diagonal

1 (14-ounce) can chickpeas, drained, rinsed, and roughly chopped

1 cup roughly chopped flat-leaf parsley

½ cup roughly chopped fresh cilantro

½ cup pitted, chopped Kalamata olives

¼ cup toasted sliced almonds

ZA'ATAR DRESSING

¼ cup freshly squeezed lemon juice

2 tablespoons minced shallots

2 tablespoons olive oil

2 tablespoons za'atar, plus more for sprinkling

½ teaspoon salt

SERVES: 3 TO 4

TIME: 30 MINUTES

One taste of za'atar seasoning, a unique Middle Eastern spice blend of tangy sumac, thyme, and sesame, and you're hooked. This couscous salad is full of luscious textures—chewy, crunchy, and soft—and is the perfect vehicle for savoring this bright, zingy dressing. Make sure to buy (or make!) extra za'atar for snowing over pizza or toasted pita brushed with olive oil.

1 Add the couscous to a large saucepan over medium heat, stirring occasionally until lightly toasted, about 4 minutes. Add the water and salt, bring to a boil, and then turn down the heat. Cover and simmer for 20 minutes, until the liquid is absorbed. Remove from the heat and fluff with a fork. Toss the dried figs on top of the couscous and partially cover the pan; the steam from the cooling couscous will tenderize the dried fruit. Set this aside to cool while you prepare the other ingredients.

2 Transfer to a mixing bowl the radishes, snap peas, chickpeas, parsley, cilantro, olives, and almonds. In a small bowl, whisk together the dressing ingredients.

3 Add the couscous to the veggie mixture and pour on the dressing. Stir well. Mound servings of salad onto serving plates and sprinkle with a little additional za'atar. Serve it!

THE SPIN

Seek out za'atar in markets that carry Middle Eastern groceries and see the online resources on page 6. Or try making your own (see sidebar)!

ZERO-STRESS ZA'ATAR

There are many formulas for the za'atar blend; this recipe is basic but includes all the must-have ingredients. There's no substitute for tangy, burgundy-hued sumac powder, and you'll need some for authentic za'atar flavor! Look for sumac powder wherever Middle Eastern groceries are sold.

Pulse the following in a spice grinder or pound in a mortar and pestle: 1 heaping tablespoon sumac powder, 1 tablespoon toasted white sesame seeds, 1 heaping tablespoon dried thyme, 2 teaspoons dried oregano or marjoram, plus a big pinch of salt.

Makes a generous ¼ cup, enough for this recipe, plus a little extra for sprinkling on freshly baked bread drizzled with olive oil or for scattering on hummus. Store in an airtight container and use within 1 month.

SUMMER

SUMMER AND SALADS ARE LIKE SUNSHINE AND RAIN, PEANUT BUTTER AND CHOCOLATE, OR DUNGEONS AND DRAGONS. SO WHY NOT MAKE THEM THE BEST, MOST OUTRAGEOUSLY DELICIOUS THING YOU'LL WANT TO EAT ALL SEASON LONG?

These recipes are the best fusion of cooked and raw ingredients, artfully garnished with outrageous dressings and inspired toppings. This summer and every summer, turn those dog days into salad days!

CHOPPED CHICKPEA ENDIVE SPEARS

 SERVES: 2 OR MORE AS AN APPETIZER

TIME: 30 MINUTES

Directly inspired by the NYC sandwich chain 'wichcraft's "secret" vegan sandwich stuffed with a chickpea filling, these tender spears of endive are slathered with a creamy chopped chickpea salad bursting with preserved lemons, juicy roasted peppers, and olives. Or to hell with the endive—go ahead and scoop up the chickpea filling with crisp crackers for lunch or throughout the day for a protein-loaded snack.

1 In a mixing bowl, mash the chickpeas with a potato masher or a big wooden spoon until creamy but still chunky. Add the bell pepper, olives, onion, preserved lemon, cilantro, garlic, olive oil, lemon juice, oregano, thyme, cayenne, a pinch of salt, and a twist of freshly ground black pepper. Combine thoroughly, cover, and chill for 20 minutes.

2 When ready to serve, prepare the endive. Slice off the root ends of the endive heads, then use your fingers to carefully separate the heads into single leaves. Use leaves that are at least 1 inch wide at the base (nibble on the leaves too small to fill) and spoon a generous tablespoon of the chickpea mixture onto the wide end of each leaf. Sprinkle each leaf with Aleppo pepper and serve!

ALMOST-OVERNIGHT PRESERVED LEMONS

Try this fast-track for homemade preserved lemons! From my book *Vegan Eats World*, a few slivers of salty, tangy lemons electrify just about any dish. Slice four organic, well-scrubbed lemons almost into quarters, leaving about ½ inch unsliced at one end to keep the lemons from falling apart. Use ¼ cup kosher salt for each lemon and pack as much as possible into the center of each lemon. Pack the lemons together with any remaining salt into a gallon-size resealable plastic bag (the lemons will be swimming in salt, and that's okay!). Squeeze out the air, seal, and freeze overnight. One hour before using, remove a lemon and thaw at room temperature. To use, tear apart the segments, pluck out the seeds, and finely chop.

1 (14-ounce) can chickpeas, drained and rinsed, or 2 cups cooked homemade

1 roasted red bell pepper, seeded, cored, and finely diced

¼ cup Kalamata olives, pitted and roughly chopped

1 small red onion, finely diced

½ preserved lemon, seeded but pulp intact

¼ cup lightly packed fresh cilantro, chopped

1 clove garlic, minced

1 tablespoon good extra-virgin olive oil

1 tablespoon freshly squeezed lemon juice

½ teaspoon dried oregano

½ teaspoon dried thyme

Pinch of cayenne pepper

Salt and freshly ground black pepper to taste

8 to 10 endive heads, about 5 inches long each

Aleppo red pepper flakes, for garnish

THE BKT (BACON.KALE.TOMATO) BOWL

SERVES: 2

TIME: 30 MINUTES

Here is THE salad you'll turn to time and time again, the perfect crowd-pleasing salad meal for vegans, omnivores, and everyone in between: a big leafy bowl of tempeh bacon, kale, avocado, and tomatoes bathed in a tangy vinaigrette. It's light and healthy fast food from your own kitchen! Awesome any season, it's especially habit forming when tomatoes are at their summer peak. Fast track this salad with the help of store-bought tempeh bacon, or make it a deluxe bacon frenzy topped with Coconut Bacony Bits (page 48).

1 Prepare the tempeh bacon as directed, then cover to keep warm until ready to use. If using store-bought tempeh bacon, slice it into bite-size pieces and cook as directed until browned on both sides. Tempeh bacon can also be prepared the night before and warmed just before serving.

2 Strip the kale leaves off the stems, tear or chop into bite-size pieces. Wash and spin the kale dry, then transfer the kale to a large mixing bowl. Whisk all of the dressing ingredients together in a small bowl. Pour half the dressing over the kale and massage the kale for a minute.

3 Add the tempeh bacon, red onion, tomato, avocado, and remaining dressing to the kale. Use tongs to combine and coat everything with dressing. Serve immediately and pass around the Coconut Bacony Bits if using!

SALAD

1 recipe Tempeh Bacon Bites (page 47) or 8 ounces store-bought tempeh bacon

1 pound curly kale

1 red onion, sliced into half-moons

1 pint red cherry tomatoes, sliced in half

1 ripe avocado, diced

Coconut Bacony Bits (page 48) (optional)

DRESSING

2 tablespoons minced shallots

4 teaspoons apple cider vinegar

1 tablespoon olive oil

1 tablespoon pure maple syrup

1 tablespoon smooth Dijon mustard

Pinch of salt

Freshly ground black pepper

EAST-WEST ROASTED CORN SALAD

SERVES: 2
TIME: 30 MINUTES

This beautiful, subtly spicy dish draws a little from both Mexican and Asian cuisine; it's my favorite way to enjoy the sensuous summer trio of sweet corn, fresh basil, and red ripe tomatoes. Check out how lovely this looks stacked into the wide-mouth glass jars on page 76!

See the tips for roasting corn on page 103; about 4 to 5 average ears of corn should be enough for this recipe.

1 Pile the corn, scallions, cilantro, basil, tofu, and tomatoes into a large mixing bowl. In a small mixing bowl, whisk together the dressing, Sriracha, and lime juice until smooth. Add to the vegetables and toss. Transfer the salad to serving bowls.

2 In a small skillet over medium heat, toast the coconut, stirring constantly for about 5 to 7 minutes, or until a pale golden brown. Immediately remove the pan from the heat and sprinkle over the salads. If desired, divide the garam masala among the servings and sprinkle over the coconut. Serve immediately.

4 cups roasted sweet corn kernels

4 scallions, green part only, thinly sliced

1 cup lightly packed, chopped fresh cilantro

½ cup chopped fresh Thai or sweet basil leaves

1 cup diced Lemongrass Tofu (page 43)

1 pint cherry tomatoes, sliced in half, or 1 pound regular tomatoes, chopped

⅔ cup Back at the Ranch Dressing (page 17, made without fresh herbs) or vegan mayonnaise

3 heaping tablespoons Sriracha or similar Asian chile sauce

2 tablespoons freshly squeezed lime juice

1 cup unsweetened coconut flakes

1 teaspoon garam masala, for garnish (optional)

GREEN PAPAYA SALAD WITH LEMONGRASS TOFU

SERVES: 4

TIME: LESS THAN 30 MINUTES, NOT INCLUDING PREPARING THE TOFU

Thai green papaya salad is an obsession of mine, and in the swelter-ing summertime this juicy pile of crunchy peanuts, crisp green papaya shreds, and lemongrass-scented tofu is a default dinner option I can get down with several times a week.

If you don't have a mortar and pestle, seal the yard-long beans and pea-nuts in separate resealable plastic bags and crush with a rolling pin. To prepare the garlic and ginger, mince them together with a knife to cre-ate a chunky paste.

1 In a large mortar and pestle, pound the sliced yard-long beans a hand-ful at a time until slightly crushed, then transfer to a large mixing bowl. Add to the bowl the shredded papaya, tomatoes, cilantro, mint, chile, and onion.

2 Crush the garlic and ginger together with a mortar and pestle (or mince) and add to the salad. Pound the peanuts with the mortar and pestle until crumbly (or finely chop) and add to the salad. Also add the coconut sugar, soy sauce, and lime juice. Use tongs to thoroughly mix the salad, folding the ingredients together to coat with dressing and crushed peanuts. Taste and add more coconut sugar or soy sauce, if desired.

3 Arrange the salad in shallow serving bowls and garnish with tofu strips. Pour any remaining dressing from the salad bowl over the tofu and serve immediately.

¼ pound yard-long beans or green beans, sliced on a diagonal into 1-inch pieces

2 cups firmly packed shredded green papaya

1 cup red cherry tomatoes, sliced in half

1 cup lightly packed fresh cilantro, chopped

¼ cup lightly packed fresh mint, chopped

1 red chile pepper, sliced paper-thin

1 red onion, sliced into thin half-moons

2 cloves garlic, peeled

½-inch-thick slice of peeled fresh ginger

⅔ cup roasted, unsalted peanuts

3 tablespoons coconut sugar

2 tablespoons low-sodium or regular soy sauce

⅓ cup freshly squeezed lime juice

1 recipe Lemongrass Tofu (page 43) or 8 to 10 ounces baked tofu, sliced into thin strips

POLISH SUMMER SOBA SALAD

SERVES: 2
TIME: 45 MINUTES

Chilled soba noodles, a Japanese staple in many warm-weather dishes, are traditionally made with buckwheat flour. While enjoying a cold sesame soba noodle salad on a steamy summer day, it hit me that buckwheat is also a staple in Eastern European cuisine. So here it is, a salad that infuses these earthy noodles with the rustic flavors found in Polish warm-weather salads: beets, cucumbers, and the requisite heap of fresh dill. White beans add a touch of richness and protein too.

1 Preheat the oven to 400°F and line a baking sheet with parchment paper. Spread the diced beets on the parchment paper, drizzle with 1 tablespoon of oil, celery seeds, salt, and pepper and toss. Roast for 20 minutes, or until tender and easily pierced with a fork.

2 Prepare the soba noodles according to package directions, but slightly undercook them to al dente. Drain, rinse with plenty of cold water, and transfer to a mixing bowl.

3 In another mixing bowl, combine the scallions, cucumber, and white beans. Whisk the dressing ingredients together in a glass measuring cup or bowl, pour half over the bean and vegetable mixture, and toss. Add the remaining dressing to the soba noodles and toss.

4 Divide the soba noodles among serving bowls and twirl into a mound in the center of each bowl. Spoon the bean and vegetable mixture over the soba, garnish with roasted beets, and sprinkle with roasted walnuts.

SOBA SALAD

½ pound uncooked beets, peeled and diced

1 tablespoon plus 1 teaspoon olive oil, divided

¼ teaspoon celery seeds

Pinch of salt and a few twists of freshly ground black pepper

6 ounces soba noodles

2 scallions, green part only, thinly sliced

1 English cucumber, peeled and sliced into thin half-moons

1 cup cooked white beans

3 tablespoons chopped roasted walnuts

DILL DRESSING

½ cup finely chopped fresh dill

3 tablespoons rice vinegar

4 teaspoons olive oil

1 tablespoon organic granulated sugar

½ teaspoon freshly ground black pepper

½ teaspoon salt

PESTO CAULIFLOWER & POTATO SALAD

SERVES: 3 TO 4
TIME: 45 MINUTES

This classic combination of pesto and potatoes is lightened up with irresistible grilled cauliflower. For a more substantial pesto entrée, replace half or all of the cauliflower with pasta, preferably those tight little twists called *gemelli*.

1 Remove the thick inner stem from the cauliflower, slice into thick 1-inch slabs. Preheat a cast-iron grill pan over high heat. Rub the cauliflower with olive oil and arrange the pieces in a single layer in the preheated pan. Grill the cauliflower until charred on the outside and crisp-tender inside, about 4 to 5 minutes, flipping halfway through. Transfer the cauliflower to a cutting board, chop into bite-size pieces, and place in a large mixing bowl.

2 Peel and dice the potato into ½-inch pieces, transfer to a large saucepan, cover with 4 inches of cold water, and bring to a rolling boil over high heat. Reduce the heat to medium and cook the potatoes for 6 to 8 minutes, or until almost tender. Stir in the peas and cook another minute. Reserve ¼ cup of cooking water, then drain the potatoes and peas and rinse with cold water. Add these vegetables to the cauliflower.

3 In a food processor, pulse together the pesto ingredients plus 2 tablespoons of the potato cooking water until smooth. Spoon onto the vegetables, add the nuts, and combine thoroughly. Cover and chill for 10 minutes to blend flavors. Serve the salad slightly chilled or at room temperature. Garnish each serving with a few nuts.

THE SPIN

This recipe uses half an average-size head of cauliflower, but you might as well grill an entire head. Pack up the leftover cauliflower and use it in practically any salad in the book, or enjoy hot with a scattering of sea salt and a squeeze of fresh lemon.

CAULIFLOWER POTATO SALAD

½ pound cauliflower

1 tablespoon olive oil

½ pound waxy yellow or white potatoes, unpeeled

1 cup fresh or frozen green peas

¼ cup chopped toasted walnuts or toasted pine nuts

BASIL PESTO DRESSING

1½ cups lightly packed fresh basil leaves

1 tablespoon white wine vinegar or white balsamic vinegar

1 tablespoon freshly squeezed lemon juice

4 teaspoons olive oil

3 cloves garlic, peeled

½ teaspoon freshly grated lemon zest

½ teaspoon salt

Salt and freshly ground black pepper to taste

SAMURAI STYLINGS

PESTO GENOVESE SALAD

Replace the cauliflower with 8 ounces of pasta. Cook as directed on the package in salted water until al dente, drain, and proceed as directed.

PEPPERONI TEMPEH PIZZA SALAD

 SERVES: 2 TO 3

TIME: 30 MINUTES

If a layer of pizza is the foundation of your food pyramid, toss this zesty salad into your well-balanced diet: "pepperoni" tempeh nuggets, fresh basil, olives, onions, and a vibrant pizza "sauce" dressing are served up not on a crust but on a robust blend of spinach and arugula. Guilt-free and gluten-free, it will leave you feeling great about having another slice, er, salad bowl. Perfect as is, but decadent with a dusting of Roasted Hemp Seed Parmesan (page 35).

1 Set aside ½ cup of the diced tomatoes for the tempeh bites. Add the remaining tomatoes and the rest of the dressing ingredients to a blender and pulse until smooth. Chill the dressing until ready to use.

2 In a small bowl, whisk together the reserved ½ cup diced tomatoes with the paprika, tamari, vinegar, garlic powder, fennel, and black pepper. Preheat the olive oil in a cast-iron skillet over medium heat. Add the tempeh and sauté for 4 to 5 minutes, until browned, then stir in the marinade. Fry for another 3 minutes, until the tempeh is sizzling and most of the marinade is absorbed, then remove from the heat.

3 Add to a large mixing bowl the greens, basil, pita, olives, onions, and oregano. Pour over half the dressing and toss to combine. Divide the salad into serving bowls, top with the tempeh, and serve with the remaining dressing. Sprinkle each serving with hemp parm!

 THE SPIN

Prepare the dressing up to 2 days in advance and keep chilled in a tightly covered container. You can also make the tempeh the night before and gently warm it before assembling the salad.

DRESSING

1 (14-ounce) can fire-roasted diced tomatoes with basil and garlic (do not drain)

1 tablespoon balsamic vinegar

1 tablespoon olive oil

2 cloves garlic, peeled

1 teaspoon dried rosemary

1 teaspoon dried oregano

½ teaspoon salt

PEPPERONI TEMPEH BITES

1 tablespoon sweet paprika

2 tablespoons tamari

1 tablespoon red wine vinegar

1 teaspoon garlic powder

1 teaspoon fennel seeds

½ teaspoon freshly ground black pepper

1 tablespoon olive oil

8 ounces tempeh, diced into ¼-inch cubes

SALAD

2 cups baby arugula

3 cups spinach

1 cup lightly packed fresh basil leaves, torn into bite-size pieces

1 cup plain toasted pita chips or Classic Croutons (page 39)

½ cup pitted, chopped Kalamata olives

1 sweet onion, sliced into half-moons

1 teaspoon dried oregano

2 tablespoons Roasted Hemp Seed Parmesan (page 35)

PLUMS LOVE ARUGULA SALAD

SERVES: 2

TIME: 20 MINUTES, NOT INCLUDING MAKING THE TOFU OR ALMONDS

Truly flavorful, juicy plums exist for only a few late summer and early fall weeks a year. Sure, you should make some jam and cakes, but why not also relish them in this simple salad bursting with the richness of gingery tahini dressing, the heat of spiced almonds, and the lovely contrast of bittersweet arugula.

1 Pulse all of the dressing ingredients in a food processor until smooth. Cover and chill until ready to use. The dressing will thicken somewhat: if you prefer it thinner, whisk in a teaspoon or two of warm water.

2 Wash and dry the plums. Slice each plum in half, gently twist apart, and discard the pits. Dice the plums into bite-size pieces.

3 In a serving bowl, arrange the arugula, then top with the plums and tofu and sprinkle with almonds. Drizzle with chilled dressing. Plum good!

GINGER TAHINI DRESSING

¼ cup tahini

½ cup water

1 clove garlic, peeled

2 tablespoons freshly squeezed lemon juice

½-inch piece fresh ginger, peeled and roughly chopped

½ teaspoon salt

¼ teaspoon Chinese 5-spice powder

Freshly ground black pepper to taste

SALAD

1 pound firm but ripe red or black plums

6 cups lightly packed arugula

1 recipe Ginger Beer Tofu (page 44), diced into ½-inch cubes

½ cup 5-Spice Tamari Almonds (page 33)

GREEN CURRY LENTIL QUINOA SALAD

Green Curry Dressing (page 28)

½ cup uncooked red quinoa

1 cup water

⅔ cup pineapple juice

Pinch of salt

1 recipe Lentils for Salads (page 49), or 1 (14-ounce) can lentils, drained and rinsed

4 scallions, green part only, thinly sliced

1 red or green chile, finely chopped (optional)

1 cup lightly packed Thai basil leaves, chiffonaded

2 large red ripe tomatoes, seeded and diced

2 cups diced fresh pineapple

4 cups mixed greens or Relaxed Shredded Kale (page 31)

½ cup toasted coconut flakes (see East-West Roasted Corn Salad, page 77)

SERVES: 2
TIME: 45 MINUTES

Take that same old quinoa salad on a Thai voyage with a zesty, fresh dressing inspired by green curry and loaded with juicy pineapple and toasted coconut. It's a complete treat as is, but you can top with cutlets of Lemongrass Tofu (page 43) for a hearty protein boost.

1 Make the dressing first and chill it while you prepare everything else.

2 Pour the quinoa into a fine-mesh sieve, rinse well with cold water, and transfer to a large saucepan. Over medium heat, stir and lightly toast the quinoa until dry, then add the water, pineapple juice, and a pinch of salt. Increase the heat and bring to a boil, stir a few times, and then reduce the heat to low. Cover and simmer for 20 minutes, or until the liquid is absorbed and the quinoa is tender. Remove the lid, fluff with a fork, and set aside to cool while preparing the salad.

3 Place the lentils, scallions, chile (if using), basil, tomatoes, pineapple, greens, and cooled quinoa in a mixing bowl. Pour the dressing over the salad and toss to combine. Cover and chill for 20 minutes for the flavors to blend, then serve topped with toasted coconut flakes.

AVOCADO AMARANTH BHEL PURI CHAAT

SERVES: 3 TO 4
TIME: 30 MINUTES

Easy Indian-Latin fusion cuisine starts with this fun salad built from purchased bhel puri mix combined with Latin staples such as avocado, black beans, and home-popped amaranth and dressed with a spicy tamarind maple dressing.

1 Whisk together the dressing ingredients in a small bowl. Pour the bhel puri mix into a large mixing bowl. Pop the amaranth as directed in Guts 'n' Glory Granola (page 159), then add to the mix along with the cashews.

2 Add the remaining salad ingredients to the bowl, then pour the dressing over and fold to moisten the bhel puri. Mound the salad into high piles in serving bowls, divide the garam masala among the servings, and sprinkle it on top. Serve immediately, before the crunchy bhel puri and popped amaranth become soggy.

THE SPIN

Bhel puri is a classic Indian street food snack (chaat), a crunchy blend of fried chickpea noodles, puffed rice, fried peas, and other goodies garnished with fresh herbs and tangy chutneys. The dry mix for this chaat, a blend of spicy fried noodles and crisped rice packed in American-style snack food bags, can be found on Indian grocery shelves. While shopping in the Indian grocery, make sure to pick up the tamarind concentrate and garam masala needed for this recipe.

TAMARIND MAPLE VINAIGRETTE

3 tablespoons tamarind concentrate

2 tablespoons agave nectar

1 tablespoon freshly squeezed lime juice

½ teaspoon ground cumin

½ teaspoon cayenne pepper

½ teaspoon salt

BHEL PURI SALAD

2 cups bhel puri mix

¼ cup uncooked amaranth

½ cup chopped roasted, unsalted cashews

1 ripe avocado, diced

1 cup cooked black beans, drained and rinsed

1 ripe mango, diced

1 medium-size red onion, finely diced

½ cup lightly packed fresh cilantro, chopped

1 teaspoon garam masala, for garnish

SALADE NIÇOISE BENTO BOX

SERVES: 2 FREE-FORM, 2 OR MORE BOXED SALADS, DEPENDING ON THE BENTO BOXES!
TIME: 1 HOUR

Salad is about making decisions: nibble on a tender potato or a crisp green bean, maybe a toothsome olive. This plant-based twist on the French seaside salad is enhanced with chickpeas spiked with dulse seaweed and Coconut Bacony Bits (page 48), all bathed in a chia seed Dijon mustard dressing. The kicker? Avocado laced with Indian black salt—an amazing stand-in for hard-boiled eggs.

I won't lie: this salad is made in stages; for the most efficient use of your time, chop the fresh veggies and blanch the green beans while the potatoes boil. But once the ingredients are prepared and packed in Japanese-inspired bento lunch boxes, your busy week will be full of tasty salad.

1 Make the vinaigrette first and chill it while you prepare everything else.

2 Scrub the potatoes, transfer to a large saucepan, and cover with 4 inches of cold water. Boil for 12 to 14 minutes, or until easily pierced with a fork. Drain and, when cool enough to handle, slice into ½-inch-thick wedges. Meanwhile, boil the green beans for 3 to 4 minutes, only until bright green but still firm. Drain and rinse immediately with cold water to stop the cooking. If serving the salad later, cover and chill the potatoes and beans.

3 Prepare the chickpeas: combine all of the chickpea ingredients in a mixing bowl. If desired, lightly mash the chickpeas with the back of a wooden spoon: don't make a paste, just mash until the beans are slightly creamy. Cover and chill.

4 Just before serving, prepare the avocado. In a small bowl, combine the citrus, basil, and black salt. Peel and dice the avocado, then gently toss with the dressing.

(continued)

VEGETABLE SALAD

Shallot Mustard Chia Vinaigrette (page 22)

½ pound small, new red potatoes or fingerling potatoes, unpeeled

½ pound green beans

4 cups torn tender lettuce leaves (such as Boston, Bibb, red leaf), washed, spun dry, and chilled

1 cup niçoise olives or similar brown olives, pitted

½ cup Coconut Bacony Bits (page 48)

Freshly ground black pepper (optional)

SEA CHICKPEAS

2 cups cooked chickpeas

2 scallions, green part only, thinly sliced

3 tablespoons dulse seaweed flakes, plus more for garnish

2 tablespoons vegan mayonnaise or Back at the Ranch Dressing (page 17)

2 tablespoons capers

½ teaspoon sea salt

Big pinch of cayenne pepper

BASIL "EGG" AVOCADO

1 tablespoon freshly squeezed lemon or lime juice

8 fresh basil leaves, chiffonaded

½ teaspoon Indian black salt

1 ripe avocado

5 If assembling a bento box, line each compartment with a few small lettuce leaves. Divide the chickpeas, avocado, potato, and beans into each compartment. Garnish with olives, coconut bacon, and seaweed flakes and pack up the mustard dressing.

6 If serving free-form on dinner plates or in big salad bowls, line the dishes with lettuce and arrange each ingredient like a wedge in a pie. Garnish with olives, coconut bacon, and seaweed flakes as instructed for the bento box. Pass around the dressing and devour!

SALT-N-SEAWEED: SAMURAI ESSENTIALS

Two ingredients you may not be familiar with, Indian black salt and dulse seaweed flakes, add a unique, deep flavor to this salad.

Indian black salt, or kala namak, is a finely ground pinkish salt with a pronounced, realistically egg-like flavor and aroma. You can find it at Indian grocers, typically stocked along with spices.

Dulse seaweed flakes—toasted, reddish-brown flakes of kelp—are popular in vegan dishes to impart a "fishy" flavor into some foods. They lend a natural saltiness to foods and can be found in most natural food stores.

If you can't find these ingredients, no substitutions needed, just make the salad without them.

MISO EDAMAME SUCCOTASH SALAD

SERVES: 3 TO 4

TIME: 45 MINUTES

Simplicity itself: corn, beans, and a splash of miso dressing gild this salad with Native American roots. Add Japanese shiso (also known as perilla) leaves for a bright herbal finish!

1 Make that miso dressing first! Chill it while preparing the ingredients for the rest of the salad.

2 Boil the edamame according to package directions, drain, and rinse with cold water to stop cooking. Don't overcook the edamame: keep them bright green and firm for the salad. In a large mixing bowl, combine the edamame, snap peas, butter beans, corn, scallions, celery, onion, and shiso. Pour on ½ cup of the miso dressing and toss.

3 Serve the salad and pass around the remaining dressing!

Fresh shiso (perilla) leaves can be found in Asian markets. They have a unique herbal aroma, but, if you can't locate any, either leave them out of the recipe or substitute with fresh Thai basil leaves.

1 recipe Marvelous Miso Dressing (page 29)

1 cup frozen shelled edamame

½ pound snap peas, thinly sliced on a diagonal

1 (15-ounce) can butter beans, drained and rinsed

2 cups fresh corn kernels, preferably roasted or blanched

2 scallions, green part only, thinly sliced on a diagonal

1 stalk celery, finely chopped

½ cup minced sweet white onion (about 1 small onion)

3 fresh shiso (perilla) leaves, chiffonaded

MERMAID'S PICNIC SALAD
WITH SEAHORSE RANCH DRESSING

 SERVES: 4 OR MORE

TIME: 30 MINUTES, NOT INCLUDING PREPARING THE TEMPEH AND DRESSING

There are seaweed salads (a popular appetizer in American sushi restaurants), and then there are crazy seaweed salads like this, melding the best of the land and sea for a massive yet light entrée. Inspired by my kitchen ninja/assistant's request for a refreshing, heat-wave-proof salad, I paired my favorite orangey tempeh with a dulse-spiked ranch dressing, greens, and crunchy seaweed for a lush, multilayered meal in a bowl.

1 Prepare the ranch dressing, then in a blender pulse with the capers and dulse flakes for 20 seconds. Pour into a serving bowl, cover, and chill until ready to serve the salad.

2 Prepare the tempeh, cover, and keep warm until ready to assemble the salad.

3 Soak and drain the seaweed mix as directed on the package. Meanwhile, prepare the carrot, beet, orange, and scallions and transfer to a large serving bowl. When the seaweed is ready to go, add that to the bowl. Sprinkle with the vinegar, oil, and sesame seeds.

4 Serve your hungry sirens! Arrange the tempeh on top of the seaweed and veggies and sprinkle with a little extra black sesame seeds. Bring to the table and pass around the Seahorse Ranch Dressing.

ABOUT THE SEAWEED

It's possible to use just one variety (wakame or arame, for example) for this salad, but for a beautiful, show-stopping dish, use "seaweed salad" mix, a blend of colorful sea greens. More expensive than single-variety seaweeds, these seemingly weightless pouches, when soaked according to package directions, expand many times over in volume and explode with a range of colors: green, black, white, and red feathery greens.

SEAHORSE RANCH DRESSING

1 recipe Back at the Ranch Dressing (page 17, made without fresh herbs)

2 tablespoons capers

1 tablespoon dulse seaweed flakes

TEMPEH AND SEAWEED SALAD

1 recipe Maple Orange Tempeh Nibbles (page 46)

3 ounces dried seaweed mix

1 carrot, julienned

1 beet, peeled and julienned*

1 orange, sliced into segments

3 scallions, green part only, sliced on a diagonal

2 tablespoons ume plum vinegar**

1 tablespoon olive oil or grapeseed oil

1 tablespoon black sesame seeds, plus more for garnish

*For the photo of this salad, we went crazy and spiral-cut the beets for maximum visual impact. You, of course, can julienne the beets—easy and delicious!

**Ume plum vinegar is a specialty vinegar made from preserved Japanese plums. A little goes a long way; just a bit adds robust, sweet-sour flavor to this salad.

FIERY FRUIT & QUINOA SALAD

 SERVES: 2

TIME: 30 MINUTES, NOT INCLUDING COOKING THE QUINOA

Grilled summer fruits, corn, and quinoa, when doused with chipotle-spiked orange chia dressing, create a fierce summer salad. Any shade of quinoa will do, but the extra-hearty texture of red or confetti quinoa (a blend of red, white, and black) stands up to the assertive flavors of grilled fruits and chiles. If you require a little more heat, toss in some finely chopped Ginger Beer Tofu (page 44) or Red-Hot Saucy Tempeh (page 42).

1 Prepare and chill the dressing until ready to use. Pour the quinoa, beans, and fresh herbs into a large mixing bowl. Keep this mixture chilled while you grill the remaining ingredients.

2 Preheat a cast-iron grill pan over medium-high heat, or heat an outdoor grill as per manufacturer's directions. Rub the fruit and veggies with a thin coating of olive oil and sprinkle with a pinch of salt. Grill the onions until browned, about 3 minutes; set aside. Grill the peaches on each side for about 2 minutes, until the outside is hot and slightly charred; set aside. Grill the ears of corn until the kernels are lightly charred, turning the cobs occasionally, about 3 to 4 minutes. Cool the vegetables and fruit just enough to be handled safely, then dice into bite-size pieces. Use a knife with a thin blade to slice the corn kernels off the cobs.

3 Transfer the chopped fruit and veggies to the bowl with the quinoa, add the pumpkin seeds, and then pour on the dressing and toss thoroughly. Serve at room temperature or chilled.

1 recipe Chia Chipotle Dressing (page 20)

2 cups cooked, chilled red or confetti quinoa

1 cup cooked black beans, drained and rinsed

1 cup lightly packed, chopped flat-leaf parsley or cilantro

½ cup lightly packed, chiffonaded fresh basil leaves

1 large red onion, sliced into rings

3 large, firm peaches or nectarines

3 ears of corn, husks and corn silk removed

Olive oil

Salt

½ cup toasted pumpkin seeds

THE SPIN

No time to fire up the grill? This salad is just as tasty made with raw peaches and onions. The corn can be lightly blanched, or look for frozen roasted corn kernels for a fast substitution.

HERBED PEA RICOTTA, TOMATOES & BASIL

GF **RR**   **SERVES:** 3 TO 4
TIME: 30 MINUTES

Salad caprese, that perfect arrangement of mozzarella, tomatoes, and basil dressed in oil and balsamic, gives me a serious case of salad envy. To further complicate things, I'm not a fan of store-bought vegan mozz. But who cares when it's easy to whip up a creamy and decadent sweet pea and cashew "ricotta" to slather over big juicy slabs of the best summer tomatoes? Don't be stingy with the fresh basil, and use the best extra-virgin olive oil and the sweetest balsamic vinegar you can find for this unforgettable way to relish peak summer tomatoes. Pro tip: stuff cherry tomatoes with the ricotta and chiffonaded basil for ultra-fresh summertime appetizers!

1 While the peas thaw, soak the cashews with the water in a glass container in the refrigerator.

2 Drain the cashews and transfer to a food processor. Add the olive oil, lemon juice, garlic, and salt and pulse into a thick paste, occasionally scraping down the sides of the food processor with a rubber spatula.

3 Add the peas and chopped fresh herbs to the cashews. Pulse and scrape into a fluffy, smooth paste. Taste the pea ricotta and add more lemon and salt if needed. Transfer to a container, tightly cover, and chill for at least 10 minutes for the flavors to blend.

4 When ready to serve, slice the tomatoes into thick slabs and arrange on a serving plate. Top each slice with a generous dollop of pea ricotta and garnish with a basil leaf. Drizzle each slice with olive oil, a little balsamic vinegar, and dust with a garnish of freshly ground pepper. Serve as is or with slices of crusty bread.

GREEN PEA RICOTTA

2 cups frozen peas, thawed for 6 hours or overnight in the refrigerator

$\frac{1}{2}$ cup unroasted cashews

$\frac{1}{2}$ cup water

2 tablespoons olive oil

3 tablespoons freshly squeezed lemon juice

2 cloves garlic, peeled

$\frac{1}{2}$ teaspoon salt

2 tablespoons chopped fresh flat-leaf parsley, basil, or dill

SALAD

2 pounds juicy, perfectly ripe tomatoes, red or a mix of heirloom colors

1 cup fresh basil leaves, washed and dried

Extra-virgin olive oil

Good quality balsamic vinegar

Few twists of freshly ground black pepper

SEITAN BACON WEDGE SALAD WITH HORSERADISH DRESSING

SERVES: 4

TIME: 45 MINUTES

This is vegan revenge! Let's take back that ridiculous lettuce-wedge-as-a-salad, the scourge of sports bars and steak houses, and make it the meatless triumph that omnivores everywhere will beg you for a taste.

This assembly of smoky grilled seitan and zesty horseradish dressing is the best thing to ever happen to iceberg lettuce. You can smother crisp wedges of lettuce for a dramatic entrée (dust off the steak knives!), or replace the 'berg lettuce with heartier chopped romaine leaves or Relaxed Shredded Kale (page 31) for no-fuss salad bowls.

1 Prepare the ranch dressing and blend in the horseradish. Cover and chill until ready to serve. Whisk the marinade ingredients together in a mixing bowl.

2 Slice the seitan on a diagonal into ½-inch strips. Add the seitan to the marinade, toss together, and set aside to marinate for 10 minutes.

3 Preheat a cast-iron grill pan over medium-high heat and brush or spray with a high-heat cooking oil (such as peanut oil). Grill the seitan strips in a single layer, cooking about 1 minute on each side to get those dark grill marks. Don't overcook, or the seitan may dry out and that's no fun. Transfer the grilled seitan to a cutting board. Once cool, chop the seitan into ¼-inch pieces.

4 Remove the core from the lettuce head and slice into quarters right before it's time to make the salad.

5 To serve, arrange a wedge of lettuce on four salad plates. Spoon the dressing down the center and sides of the wedge. Heap on the diced seitan, tomatoes, onions, and pickles and drizzle with any remaining dressing. Sprinkle with chives and a few twists of ground pepper and serve immediately.

HORSERADISH DRESSING

1 recipe Back at the Ranch Dressing (page 17)

2 tablespoons prepared horseradish

SMOKY MARINADE

2 tablespoons olive oil

1 tablespoon apple cider vinegar

1 tablespoon pure maple syrup

1 tablespoon tomato paste

1 teaspoon soy sauce

1 teaspoon liquid smoke

1 teaspoon smoked sweet paprika

. . . AND THE REST OF THE SALAD

2 Steamed or Baked Seitan Cutlets (page 50)

1 head iceberg lettuce

4 red ripe tomatoes, cored and diced

1 small sweet yellow onion (such as Vidalia), diced

1 cup pickled green beans or bread-and-butter pickle slices, diced

2 tablespoons chopped fresh chives

Freshly ground black pepper

MEXICAN ROASTED CORN SALAD WITH AVOCADO (ESQUITES)

 SERVES: 3 TO 4

TIME: 45 MINUTES

I could eat a different corn salad every night (corn is the perfect hearty addition to summertime salads), but my obsession started here: a deluxe vegan esquites, the queen of creamy roasted corn salads. Unlike most corn salads, this is best eaten when the corn is still warm from roasting, so prep all of the veggies (and the dressing, but you knew that already!) first, so all that's required is toasted hot corn for a mouthwatering treat.

1 Make the dressing first! Soak the cashews in the hot water for 30 minutes, then pulse the cashews and soaking water in a blender until smooth. Add the remaining dressing ingredients, pulse until silky, then chill until ready to use.

2 Preheat a cast-iron grill pan over medium-high heat. Rub the ears of corn with olive oil and grill each ear until the kernels are lightly charred, turning the cobs occasionally, about 3 to 4 minutes. Transfer them from the pan to a cutting board and cool just enough to handle. Use a sharp knife with a thin blade to slice the corn kernels from the cob; for best results (and to prevent kernels from taking flight), slice a few rows off an ear, lay it flat on the cutting board, then slice off the remaining corn. Always keep one side of the ear flat on the cutting board.

3 Transfer the corn to a big mixing bowl. Add the cilantro, scallions, and jalapeño. Drizzle on the dressing and toss to combine. Transfer the salad to serving dishes. Top each serving with diced avocado and tomato and sprinkle each serving with chili powder. Serve immediately with lime wedges for squeezing over the salad while the corn is still warm!

CREAMY LIME DRESSING

½ cup unroasted cashews

½ cup hot water

2 tablespoons freshly squeezed lime juice

1 teaspoon olive oil or coconut oil

1 clove garlic, peeled

2 teaspoons white (shiro) miso

CORN SALAD

4 ears of corn, husks and corn silk removed

Olive oil

½ cup lightly packed, chopped fresh cilantro

2 scallions, green part only, thinly sliced

1 green or red jalapeño pepper, roasted or fresh, seeded and minced

1 ripe avocado, diced

1 big red ripe tomato, cored and diced

2 teaspoons chili powder (preferably Mexican, such as ancho or chipotle)

Lime wedges, for garnish

BACKYARD BUFFALO RANCH CAESAR SALAD

SERVES: 2 TO 3
TIME: 30 MINUTES

You don't need a backyard to enjoy every juicy bite of summertime slaw meets Caesar salad, topped with chewy tofu drenched in a Buffalo-style hot sauce. A bold, bountiful salad that tastes even better kicking back with friends and a cold beer any late summer afternoon.

1 Prepare the dressing first and chill it until ready to serve.

2 Prepare the tofu (I suggest pressing the tofu while the cashews soak for the dressing) and keep covered until ready to serve the salad.

3 Remove and discard the root end of the lettuce, then chop the leaves into bite-size chunks. Wash and dry the lettuce and transfer to a large mixing bowl. Add the cabbage, carrots, celery, and croutons. Add the dressing and use tongs to thoroughly coat with dressing. Arrange the salad in large serving bowls and top with the tofu.

1 recipe Back at the Ranch Dressing (page 17)

1 recipe Red-Hot Saucy Tofu (page 42)

1 large head romaine lettuce

2 cups thinly shredded red cabbage

½ cup shredded carrots

½ cup thinly sliced celery (sliced on a diagonal)

2 cups Classic Croutons (page 39)

BBQ TEMPEH 'N' DILLY SLAW BOWL

 SERVES: 2
TIME: 45 MINUTES

All of these salads feeling a little too healthy for you? Then dig into this rich, creamy, crunchy dill coleslaw and sticky BBQ tempeh topped with a flourish of BBQ potato chips! Despite its decadent flavors and textures, this salad rises above typical greasy omnivorous BBQ fare.

1 Slice the tempeh into ½-inch-thick strips. Alternatively, you can slice the tempeh in half lengthwise, then slice it into four pieces, and slice each piece into triangles on a diagonal for a more dramatic presentation. Either way, it'll be delicious.

2 Heat a cast-iron skillet over medium-high heat. Add the oil, then add the tempeh strips and fry until golden on each side, flipping occasionally. If the pan is rather small, divide the tempeh and oil and fry in two batches.

3 In a bowl or large liquid measuring cup, whisk together the remaining tempeh ingredients. Pour over the frying tempeh and simmer until most of the liquid has been absorbed, flipping the tempeh occasionally. If you fried the tempeh in two batches, divide the sauce and cook each batch separately. Cover the tempeh to keep it warm.

4 In a large bowl, toss together all of the slaw ingredients, except for the potato chips. To serve, heap the slaw into large serving bowls, top with tempeh, and garnish with potato chips. Dig in!

PAN BBQ TEMPEH

8 ounces tempeh

2 tablespoons olive oil

⅔ cup vegetable broth or light-colored beer

2 tablespoons tamari

2 heaping tablespoons tomato paste

2 tablespoons light molasses or pure maple syrup

1 heaping tablespoon smooth, unsalted natural peanut butter

2 teaspoons liquid smoke

DILLY SLAW

4 cups shredded red or green cabbage, or a mix of the two

1 large carrot, julienned

½ cup roughly chopped fresh dill

½ cup thinly sliced sweet white onion

1 cup Back at the Ranch Dressing (page 17)

1 cup vegan BBQ potato chips, broken up a little

THE SPIN

If you can't locate vegan BBQ potato chips, top with your favorite flavor of spicy rustic chip. I also love topping this salad with a few slices of bread-and-butter pickles.

FALL

AUTUMN HOSTS THE FINEST SALAD INGREDIENTS IF YOU CRAVE HEARTY VEGAN FOOD LIKE ME, AND THE SHORTER DAYS AND DROPPING TEMPERATURE BRING IN A MUCH-WELCOMED SECOND SEASON OF COOL-WEATHER-LOVING GREENS.

There's the bittersweet pleasure of the last tomatoes of summer too, but a thrilling new season of crisp apples, winter squash that sweetens with the first cold snap, and hearty Brussels sprouts. Onward with fall salads!

BROCCOLI PEANUT LEMONGRASS RICE SALAD

 SERVES: 2

TIME: 20 MINUTES, NOT INCLUDING COOKING THE RICE

Black rice is a beautiful thing to behold, and it is featured in two very different salads in this book. You could add 1 cup of diced baked tofu (see That '70s Tofu on page 45) to this texture-loaded salad dressed in sweet-piquant caramelized shallot dressing, but the hearty crunch of broccoli and the satisfying richness of ground peanuts may be enough. Until you're ready for seconds!

For salad sooner, use leftover brown rice from yesterday's takeout (see The Spin tip). Grind the peanuts in a food processor until crumbly, or use a big mortar and pestle and pound them into chunky crumbs.

1 In a large saucepan, bring the water to a rolling boil. Stir in the rice and salt and bring to a boil again. Cover, reduce the heat to low, and simmer until the rice is tender and all of the liquid has been absorbed, about 40 minutes. Turn off the heat, remove the lid, and gently stir with a fork. Set aside to cool while you prepare the remaining salad ingredients.

2 Slice the broccoli florets from the stems, then slice the florets into bite-size pieces. Trim about 2 inches from the bottom of the stems and use a veggie peeler to strip away the tough skin from the stems, then dice the stems into ½-inch cubes. Steam the florets and cubes for 2 to 3 minutes, until the broccoli is bright green but still crisp. Rinse with cool water, shake away excess moisture, and transfer to a large mixing bowl. Add the cooked rice, scallions, cilantro, and peanuts.

3 Prepare the dressing: in a large skillet over medium heat, sauté the shallots with the peanut oil for 5 minutes, or until the shallots are golden and slightly caramelized. Add the lemongrass and ginger and sauté another 2 minutes, then remove from the heat. Whisk in the lime juice, tamari, sugar, and Sriracha. Pour the warm dressing over the broccoli and rice, use tongs to coat everything, and serve immediately. If desired, garnish with extra ground peanuts.

RICE SALAD

1 cup water

½ cup uncooked black or red rice

Pinch of salt

1 pound broccoli

4 scallions, green part only, thinly sliced

1 cup lightly packed, chopped fresh cilantro

½ cup roasted peanuts, coarsely ground

LEMONGRASS SHALLOT DRESSING

2 large shallots, diced

1 tablespoon peanut oil

1 stalk lemongrass, prepared as directed in Ingredient Talk (page 11), or 1 tablespoon jarred lemongrass

1 tablespoon minced fresh ginger

¼ cup freshly squeezed lime juice

2 tablespoons tamari

2 tablespoons coconut sugar or organic brown sugar

1 tablespoon Sriracha

SMOKEHOUSE CHICKPEAS 'N' GREENS SALAD

 SERVES: 2

TIME: 45 MINUTES

This salad is bursting with rich smokehouse-style flavor with paprika dressing and a mild, easy barbeque-style marinade that smothers these darling roasted chickpeas. Make this when you're craving a delicious balanced meal of leafy greens, pan-roasted barbequed chickpeas, creamy avocado, and crunchy veggies.

1 Preheat a large skillet over medium-high heat, then pour in the olive oil and tilt the pan to coat the bottom with oil. Add the chickpeas and fry for about 6 minutes, or until golden. Whisk together the tamari, tomato paste, maple syrup, and liquid smoke. Pour over the chickpeas, reduce the heat to low, and simmer for 4 minutes, stirring occasionally. Turn off the heat and cover to keep warm.

2 Meanwhile, tear the greens into bite-size pieces, wash, and spin dry. Transfer to a large salad bowl and add the onion, tomatoes, avocado, and carrot. Whisk together all of the dressing ingredients and pour over the salad. Toss the vegetables to coat with dressing and divide the salad among serving bowls.

3 Sprinkle nutritional yeast over the warm chickpeas and stir to coat. Top the salad with hot chickpeas and a twist of freshly ground black pepper to taste, and serve it up!

ROASTED BBQ CHICKPEAS

2 tablespoons olive oil

1 (14-ounce) can chickpeas, drained and rinsed

1 tablespoon tamari

1 rounded tablespoon tomato paste

1 tablespoon pure maple syrup

1 teaspoon liquid smoke (preferably hickory)

2 tablespoons nutritional yeast

SALAD

6 cups baby spinach or mixed salad greens

1 red onion, thinly sliced

1/2 pint cherry tomatoes, sliced in half

1 big, ripe avocado, diced

1/2 cup julienned carrot

Freshly ground black pepper to taste

SMOKED PAPRIKA DRESSING

2 tablespoons apple cider vinegar

1 tablespoon olive oil

1 shallot, minced

1 tablespoon pure maple syrup

1 1/2 teaspoons smoked sweet or hot paprika

1/2 teaspoon smoked salt or regular salt

MUSHROOM, BARLEY & BRUSSELS HARVEST BOWL

SERVES: 2

TIME: 45 MINUTES, NOT INCLUDING COOKING THE BARLEY

Rustic and chewy, this warm bowl of marinated pearl barley and shredded Brussels sprouts topped with tender braised mushrooms is a seriously delicious way to chow down on the best of fall produce. Fresh shiitakes or thickly sliced oyster mushrooms are a nice alternative to portobello mushrooms; they'll cook faster, so reduce the braising time by a few minutes.

For a rich side sauce to serve with this simply seasoned salad, serve with a side of Creamy Maple Mustard Dressing (page 18).

1 In a large saucepan, bring the water and salt to a rolling boil, stir in the barley, and boil for 2 minutes. Turn down the heat to a low simmer, cover, and cook for 40 to 50 minutes, until all the water is absorbed. Uncover, remove from the heat, and fluff with a fork. Set aside to cool while preparing the rest of the salad.

2 Brush the tops of the mushrooms with a damp cloth to remove any grit and discard the stems. Heat the olive oil in a large pan over medium-high heat, add the mushrooms gill-side down, and sear for 2 minutes; flip and sear 1 more minute, then flip over once more. Add the wine, tamari, and oregano and bring the liquid to a boil. Partially cover the pan, reduce the heat, and braise the mushrooms until most of the liquid has been absorbed. Turn off the heat and cover to keep warm.

3 While the mushrooms are braising, in a large mixing bowl whisk together the dressing ingredients. Add the Brussels sprouts and massage in the dressing for 2 minutes to tenderize. Add the scallions, cranberries, and walnuts. Stir in the warm barley.

4 Slice the mushroom caps into $\frac{1}{2}$-inch strips. Spoon the barley mixture into serving bowls, top with mushroom strips, and garnish with chives and a few twists of black pepper.

BARLEY

$1\frac{1}{4}$ cups vegetable broth or water

$\frac{1}{4}$ teaspoon salt (omit if using broth)

$\frac{1}{2}$ cup uncooked pearl barley

BRAISED PORTOBELLOS

2 large portobello mushrooms

2 tablespoons olive oil

$\frac{1}{4}$ cup white wine or vegetable broth

2 tablespoons tamari

Big pinch of dried oregano

DRESSING

2 tablespoons Dijon mustard

1 tablespoon olive oil

1 tablespoon freshly squeezed lemon juice

1 tablespoon pure maple syrup

1 shallot, minced

1 teaspoon dried thyme

$\frac{1}{2}$ teaspoon salt

$\frac{1}{4}$ teaspoon cayenne pepper

SALAD

$\frac{1}{2}$ pound Brussels sprouts, thinly sliced or shredded

4 scallions, green and white parts, chopped

$\frac{1}{2}$ cup dried cranberries

$\frac{1}{4}$ cup chopped toasted walnuts

2 tablespoons chopped fresh chives

Generous twist of freshly ground black pepper

GRILLED MISO APPLES & BRUSSELS SPROUTS SALAD

 **SERVES:** 2
TIME: 30 MINUTES

1 recipe Marvelous Miso Dressing (page 29)

1 pound firm, tart cooking apples (about 2 very large apples)

2 tablespoons freshly squeezed lemon juice

1 pound Brussels sprouts

4 scallions, green part only, finely chopped

3 tablespoons chopped toasted walnuts

Sweet grilled apples tempered with savory maple miso dressing atop gently massaged Brussels sprouts will change your life—or at least change how you feel about Brussels sprouts. If you'd rather serve it raw, skip the grilling and just toss diced apples in along with the scallions.

1 If you haven't made the dressing yet, now is a good time! Preheat a cast-iron grill pan over medium-high heat. Gather up some cooking spray or a little oil and a heat-proof brush (a silicone basting brush is ideal).

2 Core the apples but don't peel them, and slice into ½-inch-thick wedges. Toss with the lemon juice to prevent browning. Drizzle 3 tablespoons of the dressing over the apples and toss again. Spray the grill pan with cooking spray. Grill the apples in a single layer, about 3 minutes per side. Baste the apples with a little dressing once or twice. Flip only once and grill until the apples are tender but still firm. Transfer grilled apples to a plate.

3 In a food processor fitted with a large slicing blade, shred the Brussels sprouts, slicing in half when necessary to fit them into the neck of the food processor. Transfer the shredded Brussels sprouts to a mixing bowl and pour ¼ cup of dressing over them. Use your hands and massage the dressing into the sprouts, working for about 2 minutes to render them tender but still a little crisp. Fold in the scallions.

4 Mound the Brussels sprouts into serving bowls, arrange grilled apples on top, and garnish with toasted walnuts. Pass around the remaining dressing and devour!

THE SPIN

I've provided instructions for shredding the Brussels sprouts with a food processor. But, for the best looking shredded sprouts, I slice them by hand. Try it! Slice each sprout in half, rest it on the cutting board, and slice as thin as possible. Fluff the shreds with your fingers for feathery shreds whereas most processors only blast the sprouts into confetti.

KIMCHI BLACK RICE WITH ASIAN PEAR

SERVES: 3 OR MORE
TIME: ABOUT 1 HOUR

Icy-crisp Asian pear and chewy black rice pair perfectly with the sharp, hot flavors and juicy textures of kimchi for a sensational dish inspired by Korean cuisine. For a more complex and protein-packed dish, toss in diced, chilled That '70s Tofu (page 45).

1 In a large saucepan over medium heat, combine the rice, water, and salt. Bring to a boil, stir once, then turn down the heat. Cover and simmer for 30 minutes, or until all the liquid is absorbed. Remove from the heat, uncover, fluff with a fork, and set aside to cool while you prepare the other ingredients.

2 Chop and prepare the remaining salad ingredients and transfer to a mixing bowl, except the nori strips. Add the rice. Whisk together the dressing ingredients and stir into the salad. Transfer the salad to serving bowls and garnish with nori strips.

THE SPIN

Asian pear, like any orchard fruit, will quickly brown once sliced. This salad is best consumed after a brief chilling, but, if you want to serve longer than an hour after preparing, toss the diced pear in a tablespoon of lemon juice before combining with the rest of the salad.

ABOUT KIMCHI

This backbone of Korean cuisine typically features fish sauce or dried shrimp, but thanks to it being so crazy popular, completely vegan, high-quality kimchi is a common find in natural food markets. For this salad, drain the kimchi in a colander set above a bowl for about 10 minutes; press the kimchi occasionally to release more of the juices. Use the reserved juices for the dressing!

KIMCHI RICE SALAD

1 cup uncooked black rice

1¼ cups water

¼ teaspoon salt

1 Asian pear, cored and diced (don't peel!)

1½ cups vegan cabbage kimchi, squeezed dry and chopped

1 cup diced baked tofu (such as That '70s Tofu, page 45)

1 cup frozen shelled edamame, cooked as directed and rinsed with cold water

4 scallions, green part only, chopped

¼ cup toasted slivered almonds

1 sheet toasted nori seaweed, sliced into very thin strips, for garnish*

KIMCHI VINAIGRETTE

¼ cup kimchi liquid (from squeezing kimchi!)

1 tablespoon rice vinegar

2 teaspoons agave nectar

1 tablespoon soy sauce

1 teaspoon finely minced fresh ginger

1 teaspoon toasted sesame oil

Nori seaweed is the same stuff used for wrapping sushi. Find it in Asian markets or anyplace sushi-making supplies are sold.

FALL

ITALIAN WEDDING FARRO SALAD

SERVES: 2
TIME: 60 MINUTES

This salad has never been to a proper Italian wedding, but I adore the use of hearty farro in Northern Italian fare. This dish is inspired by those tremendous vegetable soups (known as Italian wedding soup over here) that usually feature pasta or even farro and aromatic basil. I up the ante in this early fall salad by adding crunchy pine nuts and plenty of home-made roasted garlic so sweet you'll swear it's candy (garlic candy?) to liven up end-of-summer tomatoes, zucchini, and basil.

FARRO SALAD

½ cup uncooked farro

3 cups water

¼ teaspoon salt

DRESSING

1 cup lightly packed, chiffonaded fresh basil leaves, plus more for garnish

3 tablespoons balsamic vinegar (preferably white)

1 tablespoon olive oil

6 cloves roasted garlic (see sidebar), plus more for garnish, or 2 raw cloves garlic

2 teaspoons dried thyme

1 teaspoon dried oregano

½ teaspoon salt

SALAD

1 (14-ounce) can chickpeas, drained and rinsed

½ pound ripe tomatoes, seeded and diced

½ pound zucchini or yellow summer squash, finely diced

1 cup chopped flat-leaf parsley

½ cup toasted pine nuts

1 Pick through and rinse the farro, then combine with the water and salt in a saucepan. Bring to a boil for 5 minutes, reduce the heat, and simmer for about 20 minutes, until tender. Reserve ¼ cup farro cooking liquid and drain the rest. Set the grain aside to cool while preparing the other ingredients, or cook the night before and chill until ready to use.

2 In a blender or food processor, pulse together the reserved farro cooking liquid with the dressing ingredients.

3 In a mixing bowl, combine the farro, chickpeas, tomatoes, zucchini, parsley, pine nuts, and dressing. Cover and let sit for 10 minutes for the flavors to meld, then garnish before serving if desired.

SO MUCH ROASTED GARLIC

Roast garlic cloves by the batch! Pour 1 cup prepeeled garlic cloves (common in many grocery stores) into a baking pan and toss with 2 tablespoons of olive oil. Roast at 400°F for 20 to 25 minutes, stirring occasionally, until the cloves are a rich golden brown and buttery soft. Use the roasted garlic in any dressing or toss directly into salads.

FRESH FIG & TEMPEH SALAD WITH CREAMY CILANTRO LIME DRESSING

 SERVES: 3 TO 4

TIME: ABOUT 45 MINUTES

You love fresh figs, I love fresh figs, so what better way to celebrate their all-too-short season than this entrée salad laced with creamy cilantro lime dressing? Maple orange tempeh and toasted walnuts pack in the protein and round out this unexpected fusion of harvest flavors.

1 Prepare and chill the dressing first. Meanwhile, make the tempeh and cover the pan to keep warm.

2 Arrange generous portions of the arugula and radicchio in large serving bowls. Wash, dry, and slice the figs in half and place them on top of the greens. Add the tempeh and drizzle with about half of the dressing. Garnish with walnuts and a few twists of black pepper and pass around the remaining dressing.

1 recipe Creamy Cilantro Lime Dressing (page 25)

1 recipe Maple Orange Tempeh Nibbles (page 46)

4 cups lightly packed arugula

1 small head radicchio, sliced into ¼-inch ribbons

1 pint (about 8 to 10) black or green figs

¼ cup chopped toasted walnuts

Few twists freshly ground black pepper

FALL

MONDAY NIGHT RED BEAN & RICE SALAD

 SERVES: 2
TIME: 50 MINUTES

Red kidney beans and chewy brown basmati rice are drenched in a zesty paprika-laced dressing for a lighter take on red beans and rice, New Orleans–style comfort food traditionally served on Monday nights. Here the rice is prepared pasta-style (using plenty of water, then drained) with bay leaves for long, tender grains of basmati rice. Be sure to slice the celery on a long, thin diagonal and finely dice the green bell pepper to tame any bitter flavors.

1 In a large pot, bring the water and salt to a rolling boil, then stir in the rice and bay leaves. Cook for 35 to 45 minutes, or until the rice is tender but not mushy. Drain and set aside to cool in the colander, stirring occasionally with a fork while preparing the rest of the salad.

2 Transfer the kidney beans to a large mixing bowl. Add the celery, bell pepper, tomatoes, and cooled rice to the beans.

3 Combine all of the pesto ingredients in a food processor and pulse into a thick paste. Spoon over the salad, stir well, and chill for 20 minutes to blend the flavors. Serve chilled or at room temperature.

Raw green bell peppers are not to everyone's taste; they can be somewhat bitter. For a sweeter salad, use a Cubanelle pepper (a tapered light green pepper sometimes called an Italian pepper or frying pepper) or a yellow, orange, or red bell pepper.

This salad improves with some chilling time, so consider chilling overnight for the flavors to blend.

BEANS AND RICE SALAD

4 cups water

½ teaspoon salt

½ cup uncooked brown basmati rice

2 bay leaves

1 (14-ounce) can red kidney beans (2 cups), drained and rinsed

2 stalks celery, thinly sliced on a diagonal

½ cup finely diced green bell pepper

1 pint cherry tomatoes, sliced in half

CAJUN PESTO

1 heaping cup lightly packed flat-leaf parsley leaves

3 tablespoons red wine vinegar

4 teaspoons olive oil

2 teaspoons coconut sugar or organic brown sugar

2 cloves garlic, minced

2 teaspoons smoked paprika, sweet or hot or a mix of both

1 teaspoon dried oregano

1 teaspoon dried thyme

½ teaspoon celery seeds

½ teaspoon freshly ground black pepper

¼ teaspoon cayenne pepper

½ teaspoon salt

ALMOND FALAFEL CRUNCH BOWL

SERVES: 3 TO 4
TIME: 45 MINUTES

Falafel salad is my favorite way to enjoy these popular fried bean balls, and a great excuse to heap tahini sauce all over crunchy veggies. For this lightened-up baked version, the falafel are crowned with sliced almonds for a more nutty crunch. Garnish with pita chip croutons (Classic Croutons variation, page 39) or cheat with store-bought pita crisps.

1 Preheat the oven to 375°F and line a baking sheet with parchment paper. Lightly oil the parchment with olive oil (spray or liquid). In a food processor, pulse together all of the falafel ingredients, except for the almonds, into a thick, chunky paste. Stop occasionally and scrape down the sides of the bowl with a rubber spatula. Scoop the mixture into a mixing bowl, taste, and season with more salt if necessary. Fold in half of the almonds.

2 Using a small ice cream scoop (preferably one with a spring-loaded handle for fast, clean scooping), scoop the falafel dough into balls and place on the baking sheet. Press the remaining almonds into the tops of the falafel. Spray or brush the balls generously with olive oil and bake for 25 to 30 minutes, or until the falafel is golden and has a crunchy crust on the outside and a piping hot interior.

3 While the falafel bakes, prepare the tahini sauce. Toss together the cucumber, tomato, onion, parsley, and salad greens. Transfer the salad to large serving dishes, top with hot falafel, drizzle with a few tablespoons of tahini sauce per serving, and sprinkle with sumac. Serve with a dish of tahini sauce passed around.

THE SPIN

Sumac powder is a unique Middle Eastern seasoning made from sumac berries. It has a deep burgundy color and a lively sweet, sour, and almost salty-tasting blend of flavors. Find it in any well-stocked spice shop and enjoy it sprinkled directly on salads, especially cucumber and tomato dishes.

BAKED FALAFEL

Olive oil (cooking spray or liquid)

1 cup lightly packed flat-leaf parsley

½ cup lightly packed fresh cilantro leaves

4 cloves garlic, minced

1 (14-ounce) can chickpeas (2 cups), drained and rinsed

2 tablespoons ground flax seed

2 tablespoons olive oil

1 teaspoon ground cumin

1 teaspoon ground coriander

¼ teaspoon baking soda

½ teaspoon salt

½ cup sliced almonds, divided

LEAFY CHOPPED SALAD

1 recipe Lemon Tahini Dressing (page 19)

4 Persian cucumbers, diced (about 2 cups)

½ pound tomatoes, seeded and diced

1 small red or sweet white onion, diced

½ cup lightly packed fresh flat-leaf parsley, roughly chopped

3 cups shredded romaine lettuce or assorted salad greens

2 tablespoons sumac powder (optional but amazing!)

SAMURAI STYLINGS

CARROT AND HARISSA FALAFEL

Mix in by hand 1 cup finely shredded carrot and 1 to 2 teaspoons prepared harissa sauce into the falafel dough when folding in the almonds.

COLLARDS & SWEET POTATO CRUNCH BOWL

 SERVES: 2

TIME: 30 MINUTES

Since its inception for this book, I crave this big bowl of fall-centric roasted sweet potatoes, black beans, crisp raw collards, and Sriracha-glazed pecans all year-round. This is Southern-style soul food when you're feeling skinny! If raw collards are not your thing, try searing them in a hot wok for less than a minute to brighten the color and tame the natural bitterness, but don't overcook! You'll love the contrast of crunchy collard ribbons with the tender sweet potatoes, earthy beans, and snappy glazed pecans.

1 Preheat the oven to 400°F and line a baking sheet with parchment paper. On the parchment, toss the diced sweet potato with the olive oil. Roast for 20 to 25 minutes, stirring occasionally, until the cubes are browned and tender. When the potatoes are done, turn the oven off and open the door of the oven to cool slightly. Keep the potatoes in the oven to stay warm until ready to serve.

2 Remove the stems from the collards by folding a leaf in half and cutting away the thick, tough part of the stem. Shred the collards by stacking a few leaves, rolling them into a tight tube, and slicing them into shreds ½ inch wide or thinner. Transfer the shredded collards to a salad spinner, wash, and spin dry. Move the collards to a large mixing bowl and add the black beans, scallions, and pecans.

3 Whisk together the vinaigrette ingredients. When ready to serve, add the warm sweet potato chunks to the salad, and pour on the dressing. Toss and serve immediately.

1 pound sweet potato (about one large 8-inch tuber), scrubbed and diced into ½-inch pieces

2 teaspoons olive oil

1 pound collards

1 cup cooked black beans, drained and rinsed

4 scallions, green part only, thinly sliced

1 cup Sriracha & Smoke Pecans (page 34)

ORANGE SMOKE VINAIGRETTE

¼ cup freshly squeezed orange juice

1 tablespoon olive oil

1 tablespoon apple cider vinegar

1 tablespoon pure maple syrup

¾ teaspoon smoked sweet paprika

½ teaspoon salt

COCONUT SAMOSA POTATO SALAD

SERVES: 2 TO 4
TIME: ABOUT 1 HOUR

A hearty potato and pea salad dressed with warm curry dressing and garnished with cashews and crushed toasted papadum (crunchy Indian lentil wafers), this recipe is reminiscent of samosas, the quintessential Indian deep-fried stuffed pastry. It's great anytime of year but makes for especially invigorating comfort food in cooler fall weather.

1 Either thoroughly scrub the potatoes to remove any exterior dirt and carve out the eyes, or completely peel the potatoes. Dice into 1-inch cubes, transfer to a large pot, and cover with 3 inches of water. Bring to a boil over high heat, reduce the heat to medium, and simmer for about 25 minutes, or until the potatoes are tender and easily pierced with a fork.

2 About 2 minutes before the potatoes seem done, stir in the peas and cook until bright green but firm. Drain and set aside the potatoes and peas to cool.

3 Prepare the dressing: heat the oil in a small saucepan over medium heat. Add the curry leaves and fry for about 1 minute, until crisp, and turn off the heat. Stir in the curry powder to gently cook the spices in the oil and set aside to cool for 1 minute. Whisk in the lime juice, cayenne, and salt.

4 Transfer the potatoes and peas to a large serving bowl and add the chickpeas, onion, cilantro, mint, and cashews. Pour the dressing over the salad and mix well. Heap on the crushed papadum and coconut and dust the top of the salad with garam masala. Serve away!

To roast, hold a raw papadum with long-handled metal tongs an inch or closer over a low flame until the surface bubbles and crisps, flipping and moving the papadum along the burner top until the papadum bubbles and warps to crisp perfection.

POTATO SALAD

2 pounds russet potatoes

1 cup fresh or frozen peas

1 cup cooked chickpeas (half a 14-ounce can)

1 red onion, finely diced

1½ cups lightly packed fresh cilantro, chopped

½ cup lightly packed fresh mint, chopped

⅔ cup roasted, unsalted cashews, chopped

WARM CURRY DRESSING

3 tablespoons mild-flavored vegetable oil, such as grapeseed

6 curry leaves, roughly chopped (leave out if you can't find them)

4 teaspoons mild or hot curry powder

⅓ cup freshly squeezed lime juice

½ teaspoon cayenne pepper

½ teaspoon salt

SALAD GARNISH

2 cups gently crushed toasted papadum

½ cup toasted, unsweetened coconut flakes (see East-West Roasted Corn Salad, page 77, for tips on toasting coconut)

1 tablespoon garam masala

SAMURAI STYLINGS

SWEET POTATO MASALA SALAD

Scrub the sweet potatoes, dice into bite-size pieces, boil until tender, and drain. Prepare the salad as directed.

HAZELNUT SHIITAKE BUTTERNUT SALAD

SERVES: 3 TO 4

TIME: 50 MINUTES

THIS is the ultimate autumn salad: "meaty" roasted mushrooms, meltingly tender butternut squash, toasted hazelnuts, juicy pears, and a malty maple vinaigrette (with a touch of smoked salt, if you prefer) kissed with sweet-hot Aleppo pepper! No matter what time of year, here is the salad that will leave you dreaming of crisp fall days and chilly nights.

1 Preheat the oven to 400°F and line a large baking sheet with parchment paper. Use a Y-shaped peeler and peel the squash, discard the seeds, and dice into 1-inch cubes. Transfer the squash to the baking sheet, drizzle with 1 tablespoon of oil, sprinkle with the salt, and toss to coat the cubes. Spread in a single layer and roast for 20 minutes, stirring occasionally.

2 Meanwhile, clean and trim away any woody stems from the mushrooms. Toss with the remaining 1 tablespoon of oil and the tamari.

3 Once the squash has roasted for 20 minutes, remove the pan from the oven and nudge some of the squash over, clearing about a third of the space on the baking sheet. Spread the mushrooms in a single layer and return the pan to the oven. Stir both the squash and the mushrooms occasionally (but keep separate) and roast for another 10 to 15 minutes, until the squash is very tender and the mushrooms are deeply browned.

4 Set aside the mushrooms and squash to cool slightly. Meanwhile, whisk the dressing ingredients together. Transfer the mushrooms and squash to a mixing bowl, then add the greens, scallions, pear, and hazelnuts. Combine the dressing with the salad and serve right away!

SQUASH SALAD

1 pound butternut squash (about half a small squash)

2 tablespoons olive oil, divided

½ teaspoon smoked salt or regular salt

10 ounces shiitake mushrooms

2 tablespoons tamari

3 cups arugula or Relaxed Shredded Kale (page 31)

3 scallions, green part only, thinly sliced

1 crisp Bosc pear, cored and diced

½ cup roasted hazelnuts, roughly chopped

DRESSING

2 tablespoons malt vinegar (use balsamic for a gluten-free dressing)

4 teaspoons toasted hazelnut oil or olive oil

4 teaspoons pure maple syrup

1 teaspoon Aleppo pepper or ¼ teaspoon cayenne pepper

½ teaspoon smoked salt or regular salt

Freshly ground black pepper to taste

CURRY PUMPKIN COLLARD WRAPS

MAKES: 4 OR MORE WRAPS
TIME: 45 MINUTES, NOT INCLUDING COOKING THE PUMPKIN

Collard leaf wrap "sandwiches" are a fun way to enjoy savory sandwich fillings instead of the same old wrap bread. This combo of curried pumpkin "cream cheese" spread, baked tofu, tangy pickled grapes, apples, and walnuts is wildly delicious and filling too. Unlike leafy salads, these wraps can be completely assembled in the morning, kept chilled, and enjoyed throughout the day.

1 Soak the cashews in the hot water for 30 minutes. Discard the liquid, then pour them into a blender. Alternatively, if you have a high-powered blender (like a Vitamix or Blendtec), no soaking is required: just pulse the cashews into a fine powder. Add the lemon juice, oil, garlic, ginger, maple syrup, curry, and salt. Pulse into a smooth paste.

2 Transfer the cashew paste to a mixing bowl, add the mashed squash, and fold together with a rubber spatula or spoon until creamy. Cover and chill the spread until ready to use.

3 Meanwhile, prepare the collard leaves. Slice off the stems, then flip the leaves over (shiny side down), and use a knife to trim away some of the thick stem at the bottom of the leaves. (Trimming away some of the thickness from the stems will make rolling the leaves easier.)

4 Fill a large mixing bowl halfway with warm water, stir in the kosher salt, and soak the leaves while you prepare the other fillings. Pat the leaves dry before using. You can also skip soaking the leaves; just wash and pat dry before use.

5 Slice the tofu and the apples into ½-inch-thick strips. Rinse and pat dry the sprouts.

6 Collard wraps: assemble! Spread the bottom third of a collard leaf with curry cashew spread. Heap on the tofu, apple, and sprouts and top with a flourish of walnuts and grapes. Roll it up like a burrito: fold the long sides in first, then roll up starting from the bottom. Eat immediately or wrap and chill for snacking later!

PUMPKIN CURRY CASHEW SPREAD

1 cup unroasted cashews

½ cup hot water

2 tablespoons freshly squeezed lemon juice

1 tablespoon olive oil

1 clove garlic, peeled

2 teaspoons minced fresh ginger

2 teaspoons pure maple syrup

1½ teaspoons curry powder

¾ teaspoon salt

1 cup cooked, peeled, and mashed kabocha squash or pumpkin (about ½ pound fresh squash)*

WRAPS

4 or more very large collard leaves

1 tablespoon kosher salt

1 recipe Ginger Beer Tofu (page 44) or That '70s Tofu (page 45), or 8 ounces prepared baked tofu

1 large red or green apple, cored and seeded

2 cups sunflower sprouts

½ cup chopped toasted walnuts

1 cup "Pickled" Red Grapes (page 40) or fresh red grapes sliced in half

For easy cooked kabocha squash or pumpkin, slice in half, scoop out the seeds, and arrange it cut-side down on a foil-lined baking sheet. Bake in a preheated 400°F oven for 25 minutes, or until the squash is easily pierced with a fork. Cool before making the spread.

WINTER

WHEN YOU'RE LIVING IN A COLD CLIMATE, WINTER DOESN'T NECESSARILY USHER IN CRAVINGS FOR SALAD. BUT WHEREVER YOU ARE MID-JANUARY, YOU MAY SOMETIMES DREAM OF SALAD THAT'S CRISP AND CLEAN, YET COMFORTING.

Anything to break the endless parade of heavy stews and casseroles! Enter the winter salad—a glorious teaming up of post-fall produce (cabbage, apples, and sweet potatoes) and year-round staples (tropical fruits and kale) that remind us that some vegetables never fly south for the season.

CHIMICHURRI CHICKPEAS & CHICORY

SERVES: 2
TIME: 45 MINUTES

Chimichurri sauce may be associated with steak, but this garlic and parsley pesto gets a new life as a spicy sauce for roasted chickpeas served on a toothsome chicory and roasted red pepper salad. Chicory has a bold, bitter flavor, so if you're not a huge fan of bitter greens, consider using only a handful and replacing the remaining chicory with more spinach or greens.

1 Preheat the oven to 350°F. In a food processor or blender, pulse the parsley, olive oil, garlic, vinegar, oregano, lemon zest, and salt into a thick paste. In a large ceramic baking dish, combine half of the chimichurri with the chickpeas. Roast the chickpeas for 20 minutes, stirring occasionally, until the beans are sizzling.

2 In a large mixing bowl, toss the remaining half of the chimichurri with the salad ingredients. Distribute the salad among individual serving bowls and top with hot chickpeas, then serve immediately.

CHIMICHURRI CHICKPEAS

2 cups flat-leaf parsley

3 tablespoons extra-virgin olive oil

3 cloves garlic, peeled

2 tablespoons red wine vinegar

2 teaspoons dried oregano

½ teaspoon grated lemon zest

¾ teaspoon salt

1 (14-ounce) can chickpeas, drained and rinsed, or 2 cups homemade chickpeas

CHICORY SALAD

1 roasted red pepper (store-bought or homemade), seeded and diced

1 small sweet white onion, sliced into thin half-moons

2 Persian cucumbers or ½ English cucumber, diced

2 cups chicory, baby arugula, or mixed salad greens, washed, spun dry, and torn into bite-size pieces

2 cups baby spinach or mixed spring greens

2 cups Chia Crunch Croutons (page 38) or store-bought pita crisps

¼ cup Shake-On Salad Crumbles (page 27) or toasted slivered almonds

WINTER

SESAME NOODLES IN THE DOJO

SERVES: 2
TIME: 30 MINUTES

This is my tribute to Dojo's Restaurant, a once frozen-in-time enclave nestled near Washington Square Park in Manhattan's West Village that's kept countless NYU students and an eclectic mix of downtown folks alive with cheap yet substantial eats for decades. As of this writing the entire restaurant endured heavy renovations, including the menu, which now sadly reads like any other generic pan-Asian café. These noodles are a throwback to what I loved most about the honest, filling fare Dojo's slung so well for years.

Their cold sesame noodles are not the best and are far from authentic, but nothing else will do when I need a fix. The strange choice of toppings—tomato, cucumber, and strips of nori—are unconventional but habit forming!

1 Pour all of the sesame sauce ingredients into a food processor and pulse until smooth. Taste the sauce and adjust the seasoning by adding a little more soy sauce, vinegar, or agave as desired.

2 Prepare the noodles according to package directions, but slightly undercook them to al dente. While the noodles cook, use kitchen scissors to cut the nori sheet into long, thin matchsticks. Drain the noodles and rinse with plenty of cold water, then toss with the toasted sesame oil.

3 Fill serving bowls with shredded lettuce. Toss the noodles with the sesame sauce and mound on top of the lettuce. Top with the cucumber, tomato, scallions, and nori strips. Sprinkle with sesame seeds and serve right now!

SESAME PEANUT SAUCE

⅓ cup Chinese sesame paste or tahini

¼ cup warm water

2 tablespoons rice vinegar

1 tablespoon smooth, unsalted natural peanut butter

1 tablespoon soy sauce

1 tablespoon dark agave nectar

2 teaspoons grated fresh ginger

2 teaspoons toasted sesame oil

NOODLES AND SALAD

4 ounces uncooked soba or udon noodles

1 sheet nori seaweed

1 teaspoon toasted sesame oil

3 cups shredded romaine or iceberg lettuce

1 seedless cucumber, peeled and sliced into thin strips

1 large red ripe tomato, seeded and diced

3 scallions, green part only, thinly sliced

2 tablespoons toasted sesame seeds

WINTER

THE SPIN

Sesame tahini tastes perfectly delicious in this recipe, but for authentic flavor, seek out Chinese sesame paste in Asian grocery stores. This dense sesame paste is made from unhulled seeds and has a bold, nutty flavor and a darker color than tahini.

KLASSIC CAESAR SALAD

SERVES: 2

TIME: 20 MINUTES, NOT INCLUDING PREPARING THE DRESSING, CROUTONS, AND HEMP SEED PARM

Basic but never boring: a classic vegan Caesar is the perfect winter salad. Requiring only fresh greens (romaine or kale) and bathed in creamy garlicky dressing and croutons, a flourish of hemp seed "Parmesan" adds that traditional cheesy touch that's loaded with omega-3s, or you can use your own favorite vegan parm cheesy topping.

1 Make the dressing, croutons, and hemp parm. You can make the croutons and parm up to 4 days before making the salad and dressing.

2 When ready to serve, toss together half the dressing with the lettuce in a large mixing bowl. Add the croutons and remaining dressing and toss thoroughly.

3 Pile the salad into large serving dishes, sprinkle with hemp parm, and dive in!

WITH VEGGIE BACON

Top the salad with Tempeh Bacon Bites (page 47) warm or at room temperature. Sprinkle with Coconut Bacony Bits (page 48) for maximum bacon insanity.

1 recipe Back at the Ranch Dressing (page 17, made without fresh herbs)

3 cups Classic Croutons (page 39)

¼ cup Roasted Hemp Seed Parmesan (page 35, optional but awesome)

6 cups shredded romaine lettuce

SAMURAI STYLINGS

KALE OBSESSION CAESAR SALAD

Replace the romaine lettuce with any kind of kale, torn or chopped into bite-size pieces. Pour half the dressing over the kale, massage for a few minutes until tender, add the remaining dressing and ingredients, and toss.

WINTER

GINGERY BEETS & LENTILS
WITH TAHINI AND AGAVE NECTAR

SERVES: 3 TO 4

TIME: 45 MINUTES, NOT INCLUDING MAKING THE LENTILS

The perfect salad for those who hate green leafy things: tender roasted beets and lentils drenched in a luscious ginger vinaigrette, tangy tahini, and dark agave nectar create a dreamy, dramatic dish that will have your kale-nibbling friends leaning over your plate in envy.

1 Preheat the oven to 400°F and line a baking sheet with parchment paper. Spread the beets on the parchment, drizzle with oil, sprinkle with smoked salt, and toss. Roast for 25 minutes, or until tender and easily pierced with a fork. Cool for 5 minutes before serving.

2 Meanwhile, combine the lentils, carrot, onion, and parsley in a mixing bowl. Whisk together the dressing ingredients and pour half over the lentils and toss. Cover and set aside for the flavors to meld while the beets roast.

3 Serve the salad! Arrange the lentil mixture in serving bowls, top with the beets, and pour the remaining dressing over the beets. Garnish with a generous drizzle of tahini sauce and agave nectar and serve up pure beet bliss.

 THE SPIN — Agave is great, but, if you can find it, vegan apple-based honey (such as Just Like Honey) is magic drizzled on this salad.

BEET 'N' LENTIL SALAD

1 pound beets, peeled and diced into ½-inch pieces

1 tablespoon olive oil

½ teaspoon smoked salt

2 cups Lentils for Salads (page 49)

1 large carrot, minced

1 white onion, finely chopped

½ cup roughly chopped flat-leaf parsley

GINGER ORANGE VINAIGRETTE

½ cup freshly squeezed orange juice

2 tablespoons apple cider vinegar

1-inch piece fresh ginger, peeled and minced

2 tablespoons olive oil

1 clove garlic, minced

1 teaspoon ground cumin

1 teaspoon ground coriander

¾ teaspoon salt

½ teaspoon ground cinnamon

¼ teaspoon cayenne pepper

GARNISH

1 recipe Lemon Tahini Dressing (page 19)

3 tablespoons dark agave nectar or apple-based vegan honey

WINTER

BEET BALL 'N' FRIES SALAD

SERVES: 3 TO 4

TIME: 1 HOUR, MOST OF IT INACTIVE BAKING TIME

Fast food for the 21st century: toothsome, hearty beet and lentil "meat-balls" plus oven-roasted home fries live it up atop leafy greens and juicy tomatoes. Load it up with all the fixins (bread-and-butter pickles, please) and pass around the ultimate special sauce: a creamy cashew-based "Galapagos Islands" dressing for hearty burger goodness without the bun.

1 In a large saucepan, combine the vegetable broth, lentils, and thyme. Bring to a rolling boil, reduce the heat to low, and simmer for 35 minutes, or until tender. Use a fork to stir in the bulgur wheat, cover, and set aside for 20 minutes, until all the liquid has been absorbed. This would be the perfect time to chop and shred the veggies if you haven't already!

2 Preheat the oven to 400°F, line two large baking sheets with parchment paper, and spray them with cooking spray. Add the remaining beet ball ingredients to the lentil mixture and use your hands to knead the ingredients into a moist dough. If the dough is overly wet, sprinkle in a tablespoon of oats at a time until the dough is no longer soggy but still moist. Use a small ice cream scoop (preferably one with a spring-loaded handle for fast, clean scooping) to scoop balls of beet dough onto the parchment of one of the baking sheets. Alternatively, use 2 heaping tablespoons of dough to gently form each ball and arrange on the parchment. Spray generously with oil and bake for 30 minutes, until the outsides are crusty and the insides are piping hot.

3 After you get the beet balls into the oven, scrub and dice the potatoes, toss with oil and seasoned salt, and spread in a single layer on the other baking sheet. Pop into the oven with the beet balls and bake for 20 to 25 minutes, until golden brown, flipping occasionally.

BEET BALLS

$1\frac{2}{3}$ cups vegetable broth

$\frac{1}{2}$ cup firm-textured uncooked lentils, such as black, brown, or French (lentilles du Puy)

2 teaspoons dried thyme

$\frac{1}{2}$ cup uncooked bulgur wheat

$\frac{1}{2}$ cup minced yellow onion

$\frac{1}{2}$ pound beets, peeled and shredded

1 tablespoon olive oil

2 tablespoons all-natural ketchup

$\frac{2}{3}$ cup quick-cooking oats, plus more if needed

2 teaspoons smoked sweet paprika

1 teaspoon dried oregano

$\frac{1}{2}$ teaspoon freshly ground black pepper

$\frac{1}{2}$ teaspoon salt or to taste

OVEN FRIES

2 russet potatoes or 1 pound fingerling potatoes, unpeeled

2 teaspoons olive oil

2 teaspoons Old Bay or similar seasoned salt mix

WINTER

(continued)

1 recipe Galapagos Islands Dressing (page 23) or Back at the Ranch Dressing (page 17, any of the variations)

6 cups mixed salad greens or shredded romaine lettuce

2 large red ripe tomatoes, cored and diced

1 small red onion, sliced into thin half-moons

1 large dill pickle, thinly sliced, or 1 cup bread-and-butter pickle slices

4 In the meantime, make the dressing and chill it until ready to serve. When the balls and fries are done, arrange the greens, tomatoes, onion, and pickle in large serving bowls. Top each salad with beet balls (3 to 4 per salad is a good start; you can always add more if you're still hungry) and a generous portion of roasted potatoes. Serve with the chilled dressing.

THE SPIN

You may need to fiddle with the amount of oats in the recipe, depending on the freshness of your beets. Farm-fresh summer beets are insanely juicy and may require a few more tablespoons of oats to bind the beet ball dough, but older winter beets are somewhat dry and may need a little less. Your beet mileage may vary, so go with the flow!

POMEGRANATE QUINOA HOLIDAY TABOULI

 SERVES: 3 TO 4
TIME: 45 MINUTES

Crunchy, succulent, and full of festive winter flavors, there's a lot to love with this spin on the classic veggie entrée salad, especially its star ingredient—quinoa—a rapid-cooking, gluten-free stand-in for traditional bulgur wheat. Pretty enough to grace a holiday feast table, this salad also gets a protein boost from the firm black lentils and walnuts.

1 Place the salad ingredients in a bowl and toss thoroughly.

2 In a glass measuring cup or bowl, whisk together the vinaigrette ingredients. Drizzle over the salad, gently combine, and serve immediately.

RELEASE THE ARILS!

Love pomegranates but hate removing the seeds? (Arils, technically!) Try this insanely fast and fun method: score the pomegranate along its "equator" center with the tip of a sharp knife; use your fingers to pry the fruit into two hemispheres and gently tug apart the sides of each half just enough to loosen up the seeds a bit.

Now hold one half, cut-side down, in your palm over a large bowl. Find a large, heavy wooden spoon and sharply whack the hell out of the top of the pom half, working in a circle. The arils will fly right out into the bowl (or into your palm, but just shake them into the bowl); continue until all the arils are free and then work on the other half. Pick out any bits of rind from the seeds and enjoy the fruits of your violent, but minimal, labor.

QUINOA LENTIL SALAD

1½ cups pomegranate arils, from about 1 large pomegranate

2 cups cooked red or confetti quinoa

1 (15-ounce) can black lentils, drained and rinsed, or 1½ cups homemade black lentils

4 scallions, green and white parts, chopped

2 cups roughly chopped, lightly packed flat-leaf parsley

½ cup chopped toasted walnuts

¼ cup roughly chopped fresh mint

VINAIGRETTE

¼ cup freshly squeezed lemon juice

3 tablespoons olive oil

2 teaspoons grated fresh ginger

½ teaspoon salt

½ teaspoon red pepper flakes

Few twists freshly ground black pepper

WINTER

TEMPEH REUBENESQUE SALAD

SERVES: 2 TO 3
TIME: 30 MINUTES

All the goodness of that beloved and crazy-hearty vegan sandwich—the tempeh reuben loaded with sauerkraut and tangy dressing—in a crunchy salad bowl. Didn't know that tempeh reubens were a thing? Any vegan diner establishment worth its onion rings should have at least some tempeh-based version of the deli sandwich staple.

This could easily be my favorite salad in the book; at the very least it's in my top 5 could-eat-every-day-salads. If you love sauerkraut and any excuse to eat it, don't hesitate—make this salad tonight!

1 In a blender or food processor, pulse together all of the dressing ingredients until combined. Chill the dressing while you prepare the rest of the salad ingredients.

2 Prepare the tempeh bacon, wrap in foil, and keep warm. Toss the apples with the lemon juice.

3 In large salad serving bowls, layer the cabbage, sauerkraut, apples, and croutons. Garnish the salad with tempeh bacon. Serve and pass around the dressing, dropping generous dollops onto the salad right before digging in.

1 recipe Galapagos Islands Dressing (page 23)

1 recipe Tempeh Bacon Bites (page 47)

1 green apple, cored and diced

2 tablespoons freshly squeezed lemon juice

4 cups shredded red cabbage*

1½ cups natural sauerkraut, well drained

2 cups Classic Croutons (page 39), preferably made with marble-rye bread or pumpernickel bagel chips

Use a mandoline to quickly shred the fresh cabbage.

WINTER

THE SPIN

When shopping for sauerkraut, always opt for the best quality possible. Avoid the dead canned stuff (it's been pasteurized and is lacking a lively community of probiotic bacteria) and reach for the fresh stuff found in the refrigerator case of your grocery store. Choose 'kraut in jars over bags, and over bulk barrel 'kraut above all. The pure, clean flavors of fresh sauerkraut will shine through in this salad, so treat yourself right and splurge on the best you can find . . . it's only fermented cabbage, after all!

TEMPEH TACO SALAD BOWL

SERVES: 4
TIME: 1 HOUR

Though a far cry from authentic Mexican food, taco-inspired salads tucked into edible tortilla-shell bowls have a fierce and loyal following. This one's for you, taco bowl fans: spicy tempeh crumbles (tempeh asada, if you will), creamy avocado ranch dressing, and an onslaught of cool, crisp salad fixings heaped into ridiculously easy home-baked tortilla bowls. Adventure-craving chefs should try the variation with exotic jackfruit "carnitas" for a stunning meaty filling.

1 Make the dressing first: blend together all of the dressing ingredients in a blender until silky smooth. Taste and season with a little more salt if desired. Chill the dressing until ready to use.

2 Prepare the tempeh! Dice the tempeh into rough chunks. Preheat a skillet over medium heat and then sauté the tempeh and olive oil for 3 to 4 minutes, until golden brown. Add the beer, chili powder, paprika, lime juice, cumin, and salt. Simmer for 1 minute, reduce the heat to low, and cook for 4 to 6 minutes, or until almost all of the liquid has been absorbed but the tempeh is still slightly juicy. Turn off the heat and cover the pan to keep warm.

3 Bake the tortilla bowls as directed in the sidebar; while those are baking, prepare the remaining salad ingredients.

4 When you're ready to assemble the taco salad bowls, first arrange the warm tortilla shells on serving dishes. Drizzle a little avocado dressing on the bottom of each bowl, then heap in lettuce, tomatoes, beans, onions, and olives and top with tempeh (you can warm it up a little if you prefer). Drizzle on more dressing, sprinkle with a little chili powder if you like, and serve! Pass around the dressing and a few lime wedges too.

5 If opting for a free-form salad instead of bowls, layer the bottom of large serving bowls with shredded lettuce. Spread a layer of slightly crushed tortilla chips, then top with tomatoes, beans, onions, olives, and tempeh. Serve with the dressing as directed for the bowls.

(continued)

AVOCADO RANCH DRESSING

1 large, ripe avocado

1 cup Back at the Ranch Dressing (page 17)

½ cup lightly packed fresh cilantro, chopped

TEMPEH ASADA

8 ounces tempeh

1 tablespoon olive oil

1 cup light-colored Mexican beer or vegetable broth

1 tablespoon chili powder, plus more for garnish

1 teaspoon smoked sweet or hot paprika

1 tablespoon freshly squeezed lime juice

1 teaspoon ground cumin

½ teaspoon salt

SALAD

4 Baked Tortilla Bowls (see sidebar), or 1 cup tortilla chips per serving

6 cups shredded romaine lettuce

1 pint grape tomatoes, sliced in half

1 cup cooked black beans

1 cup Massaged Red Onions (page 41) or thinly sliced red onions

1 cup pitted, sliced black olives

Lime wedges, for garnish

WINTER

JACKFRUIT TACO SALAD BOWLS

Drain one 20-ounce can green jackfruit in brine, and use your fingers to pull apart the chunks of fruit into shreds. In a large saucepan over medium-high heat, simmer together the jackfruit, beer, chili powder, paprika, lime juice, cumin, and salt. Bring to a rapid simmer for 1 minute, reduce the heat to low, and cook for 20 minutes, or until almost all of the sauce has been absorbed by the jackfruit. Pour 1 tablespoon of olive oil over the jackfruit and cook, stirring occasionally, until the shreds are sizzling and all of the liquid has been absorbed but the jackfruit still looks moist. Turn off the heat and cover the jackfruit to keep warm. Use as directed for the tempeh.

THE SPIN

Green jackfruit, a unique tropical fruit looking something like a misshapen watermelon covered in spikes, has fibrous flesh that when stewed looks alarmingly like pulled pork. Tangling with fresh jackfruit isn't recommended for even advanced chefs—the cut flesh oozes a sticky latex-like resin everywhere—but cooks of all levels can get great results using canned green jackfruit packed in brine. Take care not to confuse it with jackfruit packed in syrup, which won't work in this dish. Look for canned jackfruit in large, well-stocked Asian markets.

BAKED TORTILLA BOWLS

Wheat tortillas bake in minutes into crispy tortilla bowls. Everyone is happy, and you look like a culinary genius.

4 (8- to 10-inch) wheat tortillas, any flavor

Preheat the oven to 400°F. Arrange four 6-inch-wide ovenproof bowls on a baking sheet. Warm the tortillas (either in the microwave or a hot pan or directly over a gas burner top while holding with metal tongs) until soft and floppy. Press the tortillas into the bowls, crimping the sides to press into a bowl shape. Spray the insides with a touch of cooking spray (preferably olive oil).

Bake the bowls for 8 to 10 minutes, until crisp and golden brown; watch carefully so they don't burn. Remove from the oven and use them warm for the best flavor and texture.

GRILLED GOJI SEITAN SALAD

SERVES: 2 TO 3

TIME: 45 MINUTES, NOT INCLUDING STEAMING THE SEITAN

Grilled seitan strips all dressed up with a juicy ginger dressing, then piled high on cool cucumber ribbons, chewy goji berries, and carrot matchsticks. Clean Asian-inspired flavors will bring you back again and again to this simple entrée salad.

1 Whisk the marinade/dressing ingredients together.

2 Prepare the seitan and slice it on a diagonal into ½-inch strips. In a mixing bowl, toss together the seitan strips and ¼ cup of dressing; set aside to marinate for 10 minutes. Stir the goji berries into the remaining dressing, cover, and chill until ready to serve.

3 Meanwhile, peel the cucumber and use a Y-shaped vegetable peeler to shred it into long ribbons. Peel the carrot and use the Y-shaped peeler again to slice it into ribbons. Combine the cucumber, carrot, scallions, and shredded cabbage in a mixing bowl. Cover and chill the vegetables until ready to serve.

4 Preheat a cast-iron grill pan over medium-high heat and brush or spray with a high-heat cooking oil (such as peanut oil). Grill the seitan strips in a single layer, cooking about 1 minute on each side for dark grill marks. Brush with marinade if the seitan starts to stick.

5 Arrange the salad vegetables in high piles on each serving plate. Pile hot seitan strips on top and spoon on dressing with goji berries. Sprinkle with sesame seeds and serve hot, passing around any remaining dressing.

MARINADE/DRESSING

½ cup pure coconut water

2 tablespoons rice vinegar

2 tablespoons tamari

1 tablespoon canola oil or avocado seed oil

1 tablespoon agave nectar

2 teaspoons grated fresh ginger

1 teaspoon Chinese 5-spice powder

½ teaspoon toasted sesame oil

GRILLED SEITAN AND CUCUMBER SALAD

2 Steamed or Baked Seitan Cutlets (page 50), or 8 ounces store-bought seitan

⅓ cup dried goji berries

1 English cucumber

1 large carrot

4 scallions, green part only, thinly sliced on a diagonal

2 cups thinly shredded napa cabbage

2 tablespoons toasted sesame seeds, plus more for garnish

WINTER

CURRIED TEMPEH & APPLE SALAD IN RADICCHIO CUPS

 SERVES: 2 TO 4 OR MORE AS AN APPETIZER
TIME: 45 MINUTES

This gorgeous, toothsome salad looks great served in radicchio cups (use large leaves for entrées, smaller leaves for lovely apps), but it's just as tasty heaped on slices of dark bread studded with pecans and cranberries! Sure to thrill the pants off curry fans and tempeh fiends alike.

1 Soak the cashews in the hot water for 30 minutes, then pour the cashews and soaking water into a blender and blend until very smooth. Alternatively, if you have a high-powered blender (like a Vitamix or Blendtec), no soaking is required: just pulse the cashews into a fine powder, add the hot water, and pulse again until very smooth.

2 Add the remaining dressing ingredients and pulse until the sauce is smooth. Chill the dressing in a tightly covered container until ready to use, or at least 20 minutes for the flavors to blend.

3 Dice the tempeh into $\frac{1}{2}$-inch cubes. Steam the tempeh for 8 to 10 minutes, until tender; the last 3 minutes of steaming, toss in the dried cranberries and steam them along with the tempeh. Set the tempeh and dried cranberries aside to cool while preparing the rest of the salad.

4 Remove the core from the apple (don't peel) and dice into $\frac{1}{2}$-inch pieces. Transfer to a mixing bowl along with the cilantro and pecans. Add the tempeh, cranberries, and dressing and stir together to coat everything in dressing.

5 Peel away the two wilted outer leaves of the radicchio, then carefully peel apart as many leaves as possible (without ripping any) for serving cups (washing is optional, as you're using the inner leaves). Serve the salad by scooping it into the radicchio leaves!

CREAMY CURRY DRESSING

$\frac{1}{2}$ cup unroasted cashews

$\frac{1}{2}$ cup hot water

2 tablespoons freshly squeezed lime juice

1 teaspoon coconut oil

1 clove garlic, peeled

$2\frac{1}{2}$ teaspoons curry powder

$\frac{1}{2}$ teaspoon salt

SALAD

8 ounces tempeh

$\frac{1}{2}$ cup dried cranberries or raisins

1 red or green apple

$\frac{1}{4}$ cup lightly packed fresh cilantro, chopped

$\frac{1}{2}$ cup toasted pecans

1 head radicchio

WINTER

THE SPIN Master the art of the perfect radicchio cup! Slice away the bottom of the leaf from the core at the bottom of the radicchio head and then start pulling from the bottom of the leaf and separate it from the head.

COUSCOUS SALAD WITH PRESERVED LEMONS & OLIVES

SERVES: 4
TIME: 45 MINUTES

The stimulating, luscious flavors of a traditional tagine, that famous Moroccan stew studded with preserved lemon and green olives, set up shop in this chewy couscous salad gilded with dried fruits, nuts, and fragrant spices.

1 In a large saucepan, dry toast the couscous over medium heat, stirring constantly, until just slightly toasted, about 5 minutes. Add the water and salt, bring to a boil, and turn down the heat. Cover and simmer for 8 to 10 minutes, until the liquid is absorbed. Remove from the heat, uncover, and cool while you prepare the other ingredients.

2 Place the chickpeas, cilantro, mint, scallions, olives, apricots, zucchini, pistachios, and preserved lemon in a large mixing bowl.

3 Prepare the dressing: heat the olive oil in a small saucepan over medium heat, add the shallots, and sauté for 2 minutes, or until softened and golden. Stir in the coriander, turmeric, cinnamon, cumin, and cayenne and fry for 30 seconds, then remove from the heat. Cool for 1 minute, then stir in the lemon juice, agave, and salt and whisk until smooth. Add the couscous to the chickpea mixture and pour the dressing over it. Stir very well to coat everything with dressing. Cover and chill the salad for 5 minutes before serving.

THE SPIN

Invite summer into this salad and substitute 1 cup diced fresh apricots for the dried apricots. See Chopped Chickpea Endive Spears (page 73) for more info about preserved lemons and how to make your own homemade hack!

COUSCOUS SALAD

1 cup uncooked Israeli couscous

1¼ cups water

¼ teaspoon salt

1 (14-ounce) can chickpeas, drained and rinsed, or 2 cups homemade chickpeas

1 cup lightly packed fresh cilantro, chopped

3 tablespoons lightly packed fresh mint, chopped

2 scallions, green and white parts, thinly sliced

1 cup large green olives or Kalamata olives (or a blend), pitted, then roughly chopped

¼ cup finely chopped dried apricots

½ pound zucchini (1 smallish young zucchini), diced

3 tablespoons chopped roasted pistachios

2 tablespoons minced preserved lemon

LEMON TAGINE DRESSING

2 tablespoons olive oil

2 tablespoons minced shallots

1 teaspoon ground coriander

½ teaspoon ground turmeric

½ teaspoon ground cinnamon

½ teaspoon ground cumin

¼ teaspoon cayenne pepper

¼ cup freshly squeezed lemon juice

1 tablespoon agave nectar or pure maple syrup

½ teaspoon salt

WINTER

SEITAN STEAK SALAD WITH GREEN PEPPERCORN DRESSING

GENEROUSLY SERVES: 2 TO 3, WITH LEFTOVERS FOR LUNCH
TIME: 30 MINUTES, NOT INCLUDING MAKING THE SEITAN

Longing for a hearty "omnivorous"-style vegan meal? This is the ultimate meatless steak 'n' potatoes dish: slabs of piquant grilled seitan and roasted potatoes piled high on crisp, cool salad essentials. The creamy green peppercorn dressing perfects this salad. I could go on and on—this is one of the most hearty, memorable meals in a bowl in this book!

1 Prepare the seitan and slice the cutlets on a diagonal into ½-inch strips.

2 Scrub the potatoes and cut them into ¼-inch slices. Transfer to a large saucepan and cover with 4 inches of cold water. Bring to a boil over high heat, turn the heat down to a simmer, and cook for 12 to 14 minutes, or until the potatoes can be pierced with a fork but are not mushy; drain and set aside to cool. In the meantime, whisk together the olive oil, vinegar, oregano, soy sauce, and paprika. Add the seitan strips and toss with the marinade.

3 In a blender, pulse together the ranch dressing with the peppercorns for 30 seconds. Taste the dressing; if desired, add a teaspoon or two of extra peppercorn brine for added zip! Pour into a serving dish, cover, and chill until ready to serve.

4 Prepare all of the salad ingredients. Cover and keep them chilled until ready to serve the salad.

5 Preheat a cast-iron grill pan (or a regular pan) over medium-high heat and brush or spray with peanut oil (or similar high-heat oil for grilling). Grill the seitan strips in a single layer, cooking about 1 minute on each side for dark grill marks. Don't overcook or the seitan strips will dry out.

GRILLED SEITAN 'N' POTATOES

2 Steamed or Baked Seitan Cutlets (page 50), or 8 ounces store-bought seitan

½ pound sweet potatoes (about 1 large) or yellow fingerling potatoes, unpeeled

2 tablespoons olive oil

1 tablespoon red wine vinegar

1 teaspoon dried oregano

1 teaspoon soy sauce

½ teaspoon smoked sweet paprika

Peanut oil, for grilling

GREEN PEPPERCORN DRESSING

1 recipe Back at the Ranch Dressing (page 17)

3 rounded tablespoons green peppercorns packed in brine (don't drain)

SALAD

1 head romaine lettuce, chopped into ½-inch ribbons, washed, and spun dry

1 English cucumber, sliced into very thin rounds

2 large tomatoes, sliced into half-moons

1 red onion, thinly sliced, or 1 recipe Massaged Red Onions (page 41)

Salt and freshly ground black pepper to taste

WINTER

(continued)

6 Transfer the seitan to a dish and cover with foil to keep warm. Lightly oil slices of potato and grill on each side for about 1½ to 2 minutes until hot. Transfer to the dish with the seitan and lightly dust with salt and pepper.

7 Serve it! Shape a mound of lettuce in each large serving bowl. Arrange on top the grilled seitan, potatoes, cucumbers, tomatoes, and onion. Dust with freshly ground pepper and serve immediately, passing around the green peppercorn dressing.

THE SPIN

Tender green peppercorns packed in brine are un-ripe peppercorns, bursting with spicy flavor that gives the rich dressing an irresistible kick! Look for them packed in either jars or tins in gourmet stores, or in Asian or Thai markets.

VANESSA KABOCHA SALAD

SERVES: 2 TO 3
TIME: 45 MINUTES

After 3 weeks of photography and looking at salad 8 hours a day, I asked food photographer Vanessa Rees for a salad idea. Thinking to stump me, she offered up her favorite veggie, kabocha squash, for the ultimate salad challenge. And here we are again, another favorite make-all-the-time recipe. While loaded with vegetables, this creation is pure comfort food: tender sweet kabocha, crunchy red cabbage, green beans, and edamame swirled with an aromatic coconut peanut sauce. Don't skip the pickled ginger garnish; not just for sushi, its pickled spicy edge cuts through the richness of the sauce and squash.

1 Blend all of the sauce ingredients together in a blender until smooth. Cover and chill until ready to serve.

2 Don't peel the kabocha squash; just scrub the outside and cut away any discolored bumps. Cut in half, scoop out the pulp and seeds, and dice the flesh into 1-inch pieces. In a large pot, steam for 12 to 14 minutes, until very tender; the last 3 minutes of steaming, add the edamame and green beans and steam until the edamame is tender and the green beans are bright green and tender but still have a little snap. Set the squash aside to cool slightly, but rinse the edamame and green beans with cold water to stop the cooking.

3 When you're ready for salad, heap the shredded cabbage in large serving bowls. Top with the still-warm squash, green beans, edamame, scallions, and peanuts. Drizzle on the peanut sauce and garnish with about 1 tablespoon of pickled ginger per salad. Serve and pass around any remaining peanut sauce. Also yummy with a squirt of Sriracha on top!

COCONUT PEANUT 5-SPICE SAUCE

½ cup smooth, salted natural peanut butter

½ cup reduced-fat coconut milk

2 tablespoons pure maple syrup

1 tablespoon ume plum vinegar

¼ cup warm water

1 tablespoon minced fresh ginger

2 cloves garlic, peeled

½ teaspoon Chinese 5-spice powder

1 teaspoon toasted sesame oil

¼ teaspoon salt

SALAD

1½ pounds kabocha (about 1 smallish 6- to 7-inch diameter squash), or about 4 heaping cups diced squash

1 cup frozen shelled edamame

½ pound green beans, ends trimmed

3 cups shredded red cabbage

2 scallions, green part only, thinly sliced

½ cup roughly chopped roasted peanuts

Pickled ginger, for garnish

WINTER

SWEET & SAVORY

THIS CHAPTER ROUNDS UP THE SWEET AND SAVORY SALAD-LIKE CREATIONS I ENJOY FOR BREAKFAST. YES, I DID JUST SAY SALAD FOR BREAKFAST.

These recipes push the boundary of what most would consider "salad." Instead of leafy greens, it's all about gently sweetened grains, fruits, berries, and nuts. While there are no rules against eating any of the entrée salads for breakfast, unless it's paired with a spinach tofu quiche, I prefer my salad to be sweet or only slightly savory to start my day. Mellow and fruity, these concoctions pack a protein and fiber boost to kick off a busy weekday or a long, lazy Sunday.

GUTS 'N' GLORY GRANOLA

 MAKES: ABOUT 5½ CUPS
TIME: 1½ HOURS

There are as many granola recipes as stars in the sky; this is my star in the constellation: maple-sweetened, slow roasted until crisp, with a delicate glossy sheen on the oats. Plenty of ginger and a shot of Maldon salt sparks the sweetness of dried fruit; this is one bold granola! Sprinkled over fresh-cut fruit or berries, this is the simplest of fresh, wholesome breakfasts. You'll never settle for a bag of the health-food-store stuff again.

1 Preheat the oven to 325°F. In a large mixing bowl, whisk together the maple syrup, oil, vanilla, ginger, cinnamon, and allspice until very smooth.

2 With a rubber spatula or large wooden spoon, fold in the oats and nuts and coat everything thoroughly with the maple mixture. Sprinkle with coarse salt and thoroughly stir again. Spread in an even layer in two 13 x 9-inch baking pans lightly sprayed with olive oil cooking spray. Bake for 35 to 45 minutes, stirring occasionally and watching carefully, until the oats have a golden color. When finished baking, promptly remove the oats from the oven and transfer to a bowl, as they will continue to cook for the first few minutes out of the oven and may burn.

3 While still hot, fold in the dried fruit; the heat will steam and soften up the fruit. Cool completely (at least an hour) before tightly sealing in glass or plastic containers; enjoy within a week for the best flavor.

THE SPIN

A maple syrup tip: spray the insides of your measuring cup with a generous coating of cooking spray, then measure your syrup. It will slide easily out of the cup into the bowl, just like that.

½ cup pure maple syrup

1 tablespoon olive oil or melted virgin coconut oil

½ teaspoon vanilla extract

2 teaspoons ground ginger

1 teaspoon ground cinnamon

½ teaspoon ground allspice or nutmeg

5 cups old-fashioned rolled oats (use gluten-free oats if you're gluten free, obviously)

½ cup chopped toasted walnuts or toasted pumpkin seeds

¾ teaspoon coarse salt (such as Maldon)

1 cup dried cherries, cranberries, flame grape raisins, or finely chopped apricots

SAMURAI STYLINGS

WRATH OF AMARANTH GRANOLA

Homemade popped amaranth adds a smoky crunch that's fantastic in this granola. Preheat a large, dry (don't add oil) saucepan with a lid over medium-high heat. When the pan is hot, pour in ⅓ cup uncooked amaranth, cover, and occasionally shake the pan. The amaranth will begin to pop in about 2 to 3 minutes; when it starts, frequently shake the pan; if left on the stove for an extra minute or two, it will burn. Once most of the popping has stopped, immediately pour the amaranth onto the oats before adding the maple mixture.

SMOOTHIE GRANOLA BOWL

GF **RR** **SERVES:** 1
TIME: 10 MINUTES, NOT INCLUDING FREEZING THE BANANAS

Obviously not a salad, and not exactly a smoothie, yet killer for break-fast, a light lunch, and when I'm craving a creamy, substantial "dessert" for dinner. It's a fruit smoothie thick enough to eat with a spoon, topped with salty-sweet homemade granola, fruit, and crunchy cacao nibs. The simplest bowl is just frozen fruit, but adding protein powder, nut butter, or other goodies makes it as nourishing as you need it to be. I freeze up to a dozen ripe bananas at a time for a week's worth of made-to-order smoothie bowls! It's raw ready if no granola is added.

1 Dice the frozen banana and pulse in a blender with the frozen fruit and almond milk until creamy and smooth. High-powered blenders are great, but you can also use a food processor; occasionally scrape and mix the fruit with a rubber spatula.

2 Immediately scoop the blended banana into a bowl, add toppings, and eat eat eat!

3 Enrich that smoothie bowl with any of the following additions. Add prior to blending:

- Scoop of your favorite vanilla or chocolate vegan protein powder
- Frozen acai pulp (I usually use half of a packet per bowl)
- Couple spoonfuls of coconut or soy yogurt
- 1 soaked, pitted date, for sweetness
- Spoonful of almond, peanut, or hemp seed butter

SMOOTHIE BOWL

1 banana, peeled and frozen

1 cup frozen berries, frozen chopped mango, or frozen pineapple

¼ cup almond milk or pure coconut water

TOPPINGS

½ cup Guts 'n' Glory Granola (page 159)

½ cup sliced fresh fruit (berries, apricots, plums) or slightly thawed frozen berries

1 tablespoon goji berries or diced dried fruit

1 teaspoon cacao nibs

SAMURAI STYLINGS

AND SOME OTHER FAVORITE TOPPINGS . . .

Toasted chopped nuts or hemp seeds

Toasted coconut

Chopped walnuts, almonds, or more frozen berries!

THE SPIN

Frozen ripe bananas are a game changer. Peel, store in resealable plastic bags, and freeze until firm . . . that's it! Cacao nibs are a natural food store staple that add crunchy raw chocolate flavor without the sugar.

sweet & savory

AVOCADO & TOFU BREAKFAST BOWL WITH CARROT GINGER DRESSING

MAKES: 2 OR 3 GENEROUS BOWLS
TIME: 45 MINUTES

This savory bowl is a crazy good fusion of spicy sweet fried tofu, avocado, and Southwestern-style corn and bean salad, topped with a splash of invigorating carrot ginger dressing and a flourish of crunchy sweet potato chips. Get a fresh and feisty start to your weekend with this wholesome yet filling alternative to typically heavy, sugary brunch fare. For those ambitious types who plan on waking up at 1:30 p.m. on the weekends, prep the dressing and spice rub in advance; or don't, they're easy to whip up in minutes.

1 recipe Carrot Chia Ginger Dressing (page 26), or about 2 cups of your favorite salsa

Smoke & Spice Rub (see below)

1 pound extra-firm tofu or super-firm tofu (no pressing necessary)

2 teaspoons olive oil, divided

1 cup frozen or fresh corn kernels

½ pint cherry tomatoes, diced

1 cup cooked black beans, rinsed

1 cup lightly packed fresh cilantro, chopped

2 large handfuls mixed greens or baby arugula

1 large, ripe avocado

¾ cup sweet potato chips or high-quality tortilla chips, broken into bite-size pieces

SMOKE & SPICE RUB

2 tablespoons smoked sweet paprika

2 teaspoons organic granulated sugar

1 teaspoon freshly ground black pepper

1 teaspoon onion powder

1 teaspoon celery seeds

1 teaspoon garlic powder

½ teaspoon cayenne pepper

½ teaspoon salt

Stir the spices together and store in a small, tightly sealed glass container. Use within your lifetime.

1 Prepare the dressing and spice rub first. Slice the tofu into 8 slabs and press it (see Pressing Tofu: A History, page 9). Rub with half of the spice rub.

2 Heat 1 teaspoon of the olive oil in a cast-iron skillet over medium-high heat. Sauté the corn for 2 to 3 minutes until hot, then transfer to a dish. Heat the remaining 1 teaspoon of oil and pan-fry the tofu until hot and golden, flipping occasionally, about 4 to 6 minutes. Drizzle or spray on a little extra oil if necessary.

3 In a mixing bowl, toss together the corn, tomatoes, beans, cilantro, and greens with a splash of dressing or salsa. Divide among serving bowls. Top with avocado and fried tofu and scatter a few chips on top. Dust with a little spice rub mix and serve with the remaining carrot dressing on the side.

COCONUT CARROT CAKE SALAD

GF   **SERVES:** 3 GENEROUSLY OR 4 LIGHTER APPETITES
TIME: 30 MINUTES, NOT INCLUDING COOKING THE QUINOA

An icebox pudding meets a good-for-you breakfast (or anytime) cereal treat! Cooked quinoa, shredded carrot, pineapple, and raisins drink up the ginger and spice almond milk "batter" for a thick and tasty treat. A dollop of vanilla cashew crème (from the Apples 'n' Quinoa Bowl à la Mode, page 165) can double as "frosting" if necessary, but I enjoy this no-cook pudding plain or dusted with extra cinnamon.

1   In a large mixing bowl, combine all of the salad ingredients.

2   Whisk together the dressing ingredients, pour over the salad, and mix thoroughly to combine. Divide among serving bowls or pack into storage cups. For best results, chill the salad for at least 20 minutes to blend the flavors.

THE SPIN

Toast the coconut one of two ways: in a skillet over medium heat, stirring constantly, until just beginning to turn a pale golden shade (about 6 to 8 minutes), or spread on a baking sheet lined with parchment paper. Bake at 350°F for 4 to 6 minutes, but remove promptly from the oven to prevent overbrowning.

SALAD

2 cups cooked, chilled red quinoa (about ½ cup uncooked quinoa)

1 cup finely shredded carrots (use the smallest holes on a box grater)

1 cup packed chopped pineapple, fresh or frozen

½ cup unsweetened grated coconut, lightly toasted

½ cup raisins (dark or golden)

¼ cup chopped toasted walnuts or pecans

DRESSING

1 cup unsweetened almond milk (vanilla or plain) or your favorite nondairy milk

3 tablespoons pure maple syrup

1 tablespoon freshly squeezed lemon juice

2 teaspoons grated fresh ginger, or 1 teaspoon ground ginger

1 teaspoon ground cinnamon

½ teaspoon vanilla extract

½ teaspoon ground allspice

¼ teaspoon ground nutmeg

¼ teaspoon ground cloves

Pinch of salt

SWEET & SAVORY

APPLES 'N' QUINOA BOWL
À LA MODE

 GF

SERVES: 3 TO 4

TIME: 30 MINUTES, NOT INCLUDING MAKING THE QUINOA

For fans of grain-based puddings and apple pie, you'll love this soothing, spicy pudding-like treat for breakfast! Use both dried and fresh apples for a maximum punch of tart-sweet flavor in this creamy quinoa bowl. On cool fall mornings, try warming the quinoa right before spooning on the vanilla cashew crème.

1 Combine the apple quinoa ingredients in a large mixing bowl. Pack the quinoa into a glass container or individual wide-mouth glass jars, cover tightly, and chill for at least 30 minutes.

2 While the apple quinoa is chilling, make the vanilla crème. Soak the cashews in the hot water for 20 minutes, don't drain, and blend with the remaining crème ingredients in a blender until very smooth. Cover and chill for 10 minutes.

3 Stir and spoon the quinoa into serving bowls (if not serving in individual jars). Drizzle with vanilla crème and garnish with diced apple and a sprinkle of cinnamon. Serve with any remaining vanilla crème.

APPLE QUINOA

2 cups cooked white quinoa

1½ cups unsweetened vanilla almond milk

2 tablespoons pure maple syrup

2 teaspoons ground cinnamon

1 teaspoon ground ginger

½ teaspoon salt

1 cup raisins (dark or golden)

1 cup chopped dried apples

VANILLA CASHEW CRÈME

½ cup unroasted cashews

⅓ cup hot water

2 tablespoons pure maple syrup

2 teaspoons freshly squeezed lemon juice

1 teaspoon vanilla extract

Pinch of salt

GARNISH

1 red or green apple, cored, seeded, and diced

Ground cinnamon, for sprinkling

OVERNIGHT OATS WITH MEXICAN CHOCOLATE CRÈME

 SERVES: 2
TIME: 30 MINUTES

Humble overnight oats—uncooked rolled oats soaked in a tasty liquid while you sleep—is a cheap and ridiculously convenient breakfast. It's fun to make a different flavor every day of the week, or even elevate to elegant with a creamy sweet topping. I prefer oats soaked with unsweetened vanilla almond milk and berries, and topped with a pudding-like cinnamon chile chocolate crème, but just stir in a little agave if you need only a touch more sweetness.

1 Grab two 10-ounce jars (Mason jars or reusable, smallish jam or nut-butter jars, with lids) and divide among them the oats, almond milk, agave (if using), chia seeds, and cinnamon and briefly stir. Divide the frozen or fresh berries and drop them directly into the oats. Cap the jars tightly and chill overnight.

2 Meanwhile, soak together the cashews, dates, and coconut water for 20 minutes (soak them directly in the blender pitcher for one less bowl to clean). Pulse until smooth, depending on the strength of your blender, 2 to 4 minutes. Add the cocoa powder, cayenne pepper, and salt and pulse, scraping down the sides of the pitcher, until the chocolate crème is perfectly smooth. Pour into a glass container, cover, and chill overnight.

3 In the morning, heap some chocolate crème on top of each jar of oats and sprinkle with cacao nibs. Eat immediately, or cap the jars and consume within 2 hours for the best flavor. Bring along any extra chocolate crème for a tasty dip for fresh fruit in the afternoon!

OVERNIGHT OATS

1 cup old-fashioned rolled oats (use gluten-free oats if you're gluten free, obviously)

1¼ cups unsweetened vanilla almond milk

1 to 2 tablespoons agave nectar or pure maple syrup (optional)

1 tablespoon chia seeds

1 teaspoon ground cinnamon

1 cup frozen or fresh mixed berries

CHOCOLATE CHILE CRÈME

½ cup unroasted cashews

3 soft medjool dates, pitted

⅓ cup pure coconut water, almond milk, or rice milk

3 tablespoons cocoa powder

¼ teaspoon cayenne pepper

Pinch of sea salt

1 tablespoon cacao nibs, for garnish

(continued)

SWEET & SAVORY

SIDEBAR FOR THE SUPER LAZY!

Creamy soaked oats are perfect for the breakfast chef underachiever! You can grab the tightly sealed jar, toss it in your bag, and bolt out the door with a chewy, hearty breakfast that will keep you satisfied all morning long. I'm crazy about my chocolate crème oat parfaits, but you'll get equally satisfying everyday results if you leave it out.

For less-dessert-like oats, replace the chocolate crème with a big dollop of nut butter packed directly into the bottom of the jar. Right before eating, stir the jar for a boost of nutty protein. For each serving, start with 6- to 8-ounce Mason jars (look for these in hardware stores or even Whole Foods). These are really small jars!

PER JAR:

- · 1 tablespoon almond, cashew, or other nut butter
- · ½ cup old-fashioned rolled oats
- · 1 teaspoon chia seeds or ground flax seeds
- · ½ cup unsweetened vanilla almond milk
- · 1 tablespoon raisins, dried cherries, cranberries, or other favorite dried fruit
- · ¼ cup blueberries, raspberries, diced strawberries, or diced peaches, fresh or frozen
- · 2 tablespoons chopped toasted walnuts or pecans
- · Ground cinnamon and/or coconut sugar (optional)

1 Drop the nut butter into the jar and mash it down with the back of a spoon.

2 Add the oats and flax seeds and pour on the almond milk. Drop in any fresh, dried, and frozen fruit, then the nuts, and dust the top with a pinch of cinnamon and/or coconut sugar, if desired. Seal tightly and chill overnight. Stir before eating!

ORANGE VANILLA FRUIT CUPS

GF **RR** **SERVES:** 4
TIME: 15 MINUTES

3 cups freshly squeezed
or store-bought orange juice

2 tablespoons freshly squeezed
lime juice

1 tablespoon agave nectar

½ teaspoon vanilla extract

2 large nectarines

2 large red plums

1 large green apple

1 cup seedless green grapes

1 pint blueberries

A childhood favorite of mine, this salad never had a proper name, only "the orange juice salad." My parents and I ate endless amounts of it during that time of year when the pavement sizzled and nobody dared to turn on the stove. According to my mother it's a Venezuelan specialty—fresh chunks of summer fruit swimming in orange juice—but I'll always think of humid New England summers spent sipping the fruity juices from the bottom of the bowl. Favorite way to eat it: ladled into a big mug, with a spoon handy for snacking while catching up on summer reading.

My modern version gilds the orange juice with a touch of lime juice, agave nectar, and vanilla extract, but the fruit selection is nearly the same. Change the fruit as the seasonal selection shifts: tiny plums instead of nectarines, and skip the grapes if blueberries are on sale. Sometimes we'd throw in a diced banana or some sliced strawberries, but, after a day of soaking in juice, these can get a little soggy, so consider yourself warned.

SAMURAI STYLINGS

ORANGE CRÈME CUPS

Top each cup with a big dollop of vanilla coconut yogurt right before serving!

1 In a 2-quart glass or plastic pitcher, whisk together the orange juice, lime juice, agave nectar, and vanilla extract.

2 Remove the cores and seeds from the nectarines, plums, and apple. Slice the fruit into bite-size pieces, transferring the fruit chunks directly into the orange juice as you slice them. Slice the grapes in half and add those along with the whole blueberries into the juice. Cover and chill for 30 minutes, then ladle the fruit and juice into large mugs and serve with a spoon.

THANKS AND ACKNOWLEDGMENTS

Cookbooks and salads are both the sum of many delicious, essential components working in harmony. Endless thanks and praise to the fresh folks who helped me make this book, which I hope will nourish and inspire you for many meals to come:

- John Stavropolous, my partner in all things in salad and in life, and the Stavropolous family

- My parents, Teresa and Nerio

- Timberly Stevens, arch recipe tester and kitchen ninja

- Vanessa Rees, photographer-stylist sensei, Roy Rogers for much appreciated coffee runs, and Marshall the cat, for ear scratching and belly rubs on demand (demanded from us, that is)

- The wise and quick-like-a-bunny team at Da Capo: my editor Renee Sedliar, Jonathan Sainsbury, Amber Morris, Katie Wilson, and Kevin Hanover

- My agent Marc Gerald and The Agency

And a cast of friends and colleagues who supported me during the twists and turns of this tour de salad: Isa Chandra Moskowitz (cookbook sisters 4 life), Ajit George (samurai!), Lizzie Stark (very different books but same dread deadline), George Locke, James Stuart, Jared Sorenson, Luke Crane, Dro, Creative Wednesdays Warriors (Dev, Laura, Sara), The Vegan Mashup (Betsy Carson, Toni Fiore, Miyoko Schinner), Adam Sobel and the Cinnamon Snail funky bunch, the Community Team @ Kickstarter (Cindy, Aurora, Niina, Callan, Jamie, John, Julio, George, Liz, Nicole, everyone else on the Community Team, and Sam [still working on that brogrammer salad]), and all the salad ninjas who believe that Salads Don't Suck.

METRIC CONVERSIONS

- The recipes in this book have not been tested with metric measurements, so some variations might occur.

- Remember that the weight of dry ingredients varies according to the volume or density factor: 1 cup of flour weighs far less than 1 cup of sugar, and 1 tablespoon doesn't necessarily hold 3 teaspoons.

GENERAL FORMULA FOR METRIC CONVERSION

Ounces to grams	ounces × 28.35 = grams
Grams to ounces	grams × 0.035 = ounces
Pounds to grams	pounds × 453.5 = grams
Pounds to kilograms	pounds × 0.45 = kilograms
Cups to liters	cups × 0.24 = liters
Fahrenheit to Celsius	(°F − 32) × 5 ÷ 9 = °C
Celsius to Fahrenheit	(°C × 9) ÷ 5 + 32 = °F

VOLUME (LIQUID) MEASUREMENTS

1 teaspoon = 1/6 fluid ounce = 5 milliliters

1 tablespoon = 1/2 fluid ounce = 15 milliliters

2 tablespoons = 1 fluid ounce = 30 milliliters

1/4 cup = 2 fluid ounces = 60 milliliters

1/3 cup = 2 2/3 fluid ounces = 79 milliliters

1/2 cup = 4 fluid ounces = 118 milliliters

1 cup or 1/2 pint = 8 fluid ounces = 250 milliliters

2 cups or 1 pint = 16 fluid ounces = 500 milliliters

4 cups or 1 quart = 32 fluid ounces = 1,000 milliliters

1 gallon = 4 liters

VOLUME (DRY) MEASUREMENTS

1/4 teaspoon = 1 milliliter

1/2 teaspoon = 2 milliliters

3/4 teaspoon = 4 milliliters

1 teaspoon = 5 milliliters

1 tablespoon = 15 milliliters

1/4 cup = 59 milliliters

1/3 cup = 79 milliliters

1/2 cup = 118 milliliters

2/3 cup = 158 milliliters

3/4 cup = 177 milliliters

1 cup = 225 milliliters

4 cups or 1 quart = 1 liter

1/2 gallon = 2 liters

1 gallon = 4 liters

OVEN TEMPERATURE EQUIVALENTS, FAHRENHEIT (F) AND CELSIUS (C)

100°F = 38°C

200°F = 95°C

250°F = 120°C

300°F = 150°C

350°F = 180°C

400°F = 205°C

450°F = 230°C

WEIGHT (MASS) MEASUREMENTS

1 ounce = 30 grams

2 ounces = 55 grams

3 ounces = 85 grams

4 ounces = 1/4 pound = 125 grams

8 ounces = 1/2 pound = 240 grams

12 ounces = 3/4 pound = 375 grams

16 ounces = 1 pound = 454 grams

LINEAR MEASUREMENTS

1/2 in = 1 1/2 cm

1 inch = 2 1/2 cm

6 inches = 15 cm

8 inches = 20 cm

10 inches = 25 cm

12 inches = 30 cm

20 inches = 50 cm

INDEX